ISBN-13: 978-1790197804

Always for the sake of the Almighty One, Who is The Reality of All Mirrors of Gratitude!

And to that Perfect Mirror, the principle of praise and beauty ... Muhammad!

And to the Sultan of Saints and my heart's succor, Mevlana Shaykh Nazim ... You grabbed me from the desert of forms to the dessert of heavenly norms!

And to my Muhammadan Pole of Power and Grace, Mevlana Shaykh Hisham! In your presence, I'm with the Hashemite King.

And to my spiritual mothers, Hajjah Amina and Hajjah Naziha, your Amana and Nazaha engulf us in the purity of al-Zahra!

And to my parents, Zohair and Sawsan, you are the roses of my heart and wings with which I fly.

And to my Fatima Zahra ... with you I'm complete; you are who I want to be!

Contents

Prelude

A place is a piece of the whole environment
that has been claimed by feelings.
- Alan Gussow, "A Sense of Place"

This began as an inspiration to write a story of Sufism, a biography for an entity without a body or, inversely, one that has infinite bodies. As I began to write whatever came to my heart, as opposed to mind, I found myself writing my own story. I realized, then and there, that a biography – amongst many – of Sufism can only emerge through the intimate experiences of a love and through the taste of the mundane, not necessarily the glorious or religious.

As I continued to write, I discovered that this autobiography is not really concerned with human bodies as much as architectural effigies. This is an autobiography that traces not the fate of human bodies, conversations or monologues. It is a history of places, spaces and textures. You should *not* expect to find many conversations between friends or the usual coming-to-be fruitions of human realizations. Rather, I ask you to listen instead to the whispers of ambiances and how they tell their stories and communicate connections, through me as their observing narrator, with other places and spaces elsewhere in this book.

This type of autobiography would not be possible without a reliance and constant awareness of the two wings of *nostalgia*: memory and imagination. The conversations I construct between homes, kitchens, castles and promenades are an homage to the workings of this *nostalgia* in my own memory; how it subdues the imagination and forces it to alter and embellish memories from the past … entirely for the beautiful purpose that they continue living and surviving in a tumultuous present of diaspora and migration.

The effects of this alteration can be felt most clearly in the some 'intentional' mistakes which I have left intact. For instance, I recently found out from my parents that our last apartment in Amman was not, in fact, located in Gardens. However, since my imagination has decided that it WAS located in that luxurious and busy street, I have decided to leave it in peace.

Also in the course of writing this book, I decided that it should be the first volume, titled "Childhood Between Rivers and mountains" of a trilogy where I share the souk of my life's nostalgia with you, the reader. In this first book, I journey with through the first decade of my life, beginning in the land between two rivers, Iraq and culminating with the following six years in Jordan. All the while, I share with you the effects that war, diaspora and migration have had on the physical places I lived in and their current traces in my imagination.

Volumes 2 and 3 of the *Souk of Nostalgia*, still to be written, will explore the spiritual attachment I have to my motherly ancestor, Egypt, and eventual migration to America, leading to the present reflections on this rather young past of thirty years mired in not so brief transitions and separations.

Part I: Overture
The Birth of Memories and Bodies

One can speak best through stories. Things only come alive in this way. This is because such things are the children of our experiences. They are conceived during big events in our lives, born when we begin to reflect on those incidents and then grow with us as our appreciation for the memories that brought them into being also lives and thrives.

I think human life is best described as art, and these children of our experiences are like the brush strokes on the canvas of our existence. Different colors and their contrasting arrangements somehow always create a sense of harmony and aesthetic love in the observer. On the other hand, an empty canvas is either an unborn life or a unique delicacy. Either way, you and I would not be able to live in such a canvas, with a brush stroke of one single color.

But why do colors need each other? And why do we need varying experiences in our lives? Because colors know one another in the other. Blues thrive in their unique hue best when surrounded by reds and greens. Likewise, white and black remind the onlooker of their singular selves, as the beginning emptiness and eventual culmination of all colors. Similarly, experiences in our lives and their memories are like mirrors wherein we can reflect upon our previous selves, and continue to find out the abyss of our infinite essence.

Perhaps this is what drove me, while submitting my application for graduate studies, to describe myself as a child born from the marriage of three oceans, Iraqi, Egyptian and Muslim. I was gifted this metaphor by the famed Egyptian Novelist Naguib Mahfouz, who also pronounced his story as a child born from the marriage between Ancient Egypt and Islam. This was part of his address to the Nobel Prize association, when they chose to gift him the prestigious award.

The difference between me and Mahfouz is that he never left Egypt, while I only lived in my country of birth, Iraq, for the first six years of my life. However, our lives converge as I reach my thirties and only now begin to grasp and appreciate the complex yet elusively perfect harmony of human existence. The paragon of Arabic literature Mahfouz gleaned these timeless brush strokes already at a young age from the intricate daily spirit of the old neighborhoods of Cairo. On the other hand, I only sensed their presence later on in life, across vast distances and changing time zones.

Part II: Origins
A Palace on Haifa Street

This journey began in Iraq in 1984, amidst my country's war with Iran. I have no recollection of that event which nearly lasted a decade, save what my parents tell me of its seemingly nonexistent effect on life in Baghdad, my city of birth. Certainly, Iraqis and people of other countries in the region had gone through their share of warfare since time immemorial, and they perhaps sensed that this war would not be the last to touch their lives, so they continued to live.

I have very few but vivid images from my childhood in this *bilad al-Rafidayn* (The Land between two Rivers). I remember waiting for the school bus across my apartment building and recall having to walk some 3-4 miles home one day because the bus broke down. Another picture now comes of a vast courtyard of marble nearby our house with a nice strip mall. I see myself walking there with friends after school.

Of course, there are always memories of getting sick at school and waiting for your parents to pick you up. Yet, as the years passed, the individualism of each image dissipates and what becomes more important are the relationships and stories that clothed themselves in those memories. The modern appeal of our apartment, built by European architects, in Haifa street, has a color hue much different than the traditional aging home of my grandparents in the Karrada neighborhood, hugging the riverbank.

As I write this, however, there is no distinction: both the modern and traditional become ancient in the desert of my memory. Still, such places, events and people from the past tend to remain fresh when they reside in treasuries of past imagination. It is as if they are released from their historical bodies and can fly freely, upon the death of their moment, in a timeless spiritual ocean. It is almost a paralyzing paradox, how these figments from the past sustain themselves on the misery of our distance from their original forms, from the moments they entered our lives long ago.

Melancholy nostalgia is a grand artist's inspiration as they gaze upon the canvas of their spirit. I keep this in mind as I try to maintain an eternal tango with my past. The First Gulf War would be the initial splash of new colors to enter my portrait. During its moment, when that new hue infiltrated my surroundings, I could only sense the shock of the instant; the appreciation of the tone and pitch of the color only arrived much later.

I can still see buildings turned inside out, while just the day before they were prudently rooted. Though, such ruptures of normal life are part and parcel of existence, but we don't notice. Ask the trees about their leaves, they know to enjoy their company in the spring and prepare for their demise when the throngs of fall appear. Winter then comes as a slumber to bury the deceased under the coolness of snow and await the second coming.

The spirit of the reflection is that falling leaves hide a tremendous life behind their demise; and beyond the destruction of my city of Baghdad there is a new spiritual spring waiting to gush forth. It's a subtle vision that requires much patience. Not a passive awaiting, but rather an active act of listening for the creative arrival that is always imminent.

This spiritual gift of war is precisely the unrehearsed distance and descent from normalcy into a life of transition. The trauma of sound, movement and uncertainty that accompanies war creates an open wound that hearkens for healing obtainable only through creativity. Not a superficial emptying of words on paper or brush strokes on canvas, but rather an act of imitative art that shadows the movements of stars as they course through their vast distances to their last recourse, the final destination.

And yet, there is more. The trees without their leaves are in a naked pure life. So blunt in their primordial nature that it frightens those of us who are used to form and tainted origins. That image of a trunk with thirsty wooden branches is a memory of our essence without the body's clothing. War, similarly, lifts the façade off corruption; it brings to the forefront the passing of forms and the concurrent miraculous nature of their subsistence.

And thus, we got used to the war sirens and empty apartment of our neighbors next door. Everyone fled their home towards uncertainty and their abodes were new once again, waiting for new tenants. I sometimes wonder whether furniture that we use daily knows it's under temporary ownership, eventually to be sold or gifted to new masters due to unforeseen circumstances.

I say this because the sudden emptiness next door began to corrode the vibrant corners of our house. It was like an inevitable warning: "you will leave your home as well, this is not like the last war … this is unrelenting change!" Even though our neighbors returned to their house some weeks later, there was no reversal to this epidemic affecting the ambiance.

I necessarily have to impose a rewriting of the narrative of this war in my memory, and try to recreate new props and setting for the looming changes to come. I remember a dismemberment of familial familiarity, of friends and relatives gathering together in our spacious living room that, in my imagination, is erected as a palace. Our kitchen rivaled, in its detail, delicacies found in the rich alleyways of Paris while our balcony was an architectural spring that constantly revived every atom of our house with Baghdadian breezes.

As for the rest of the place, the corridor from the living room and kitchen to my parents' bedroom seems now to stretch to eternity. The two other bedrooms, for my siblings and I, connect through this hallway with my parents' private space as two wings of a gracious bird. I can still see my sister's posters of George Michael hanging on the walls of our bedroom; they reminisce of that 80's musical life. Meanwhile, I stand in the hallway playing with my toy gun or trying to fly my miniature helicopter.

These now refurbished memories have smells and hues associated with them. They seem to glow as they sustain my creative nostalgia for a distant time and place. All of a sudden, the war seems to have abolished that luster, in favor of sirens of war that sound in the horizon, which now force themselves through our balcony after overthrowing the governance of that ancient Mesopotamian breeze ... they also reveal with their suddenness an age of uncertainty to come.

And so, this new era of doubt, brought upon us by the sirens of war, killed the old vibrancy of hues and smells, which naturally required peace and tradition to emerge over time. Now, even the whiteness of our living room seems dead as we eat a quick meal that was cooked in fear of losing electricity. Incidentally, the only peaceful memory in this age of war seems to be an ecstatic proclamation of fake victory when electricity returned, after months of darkness due to the bombing. This occurs also after electricity was a granted luxury in the lives of Iraqis before the invasion; as granted as the sun's generosity.

Eventually, the desertion of smells, hues and luminous energy was followed by us moving from our apartment in Haifa street to my grandparents' house in the Karrada neighborhood. That would be the last I ever see of that spacious white palace with my own eyes and final reservoir of memories that I can discuss of its hospitality. From then on, my stay in Baghdad was breathing its last in a house that itself was aging and spoke of a wrinkled sadness and its own foreboding death.

An Aging Castle in Karrada

If our apartment in Haifa street was a white palace, then my grandparents' abode was an ancient castle that rivaled the fortresses of Europe as it withstood the test of time. Its age and brittle walls also have their share of generous artistic memories to speak about. My grandmother's kitchen did not care to rival Parisian cuisines, but rather settled for lighting the fire under pots and pans whose taste and smells can even awaken homeliness and generosity from their slumber.

The living room, with its traditional seating arrangement of classical brown and reddish hues narrate the entire history of Iraq through their worn threads. My grandfather's private room overlooks both the old street and garden which we will discuss momentarily. His antique wall clock, with naturally smelling wood, worked without batteries. It reminisces of a time when people lived through their constant inner movement, without need for resuscitating technology.

As for the house's garden, it requires its own stories and narratives to give it its due right. Almost always, when the memories of Iraq and the neighborhood of Karrada visit me, they all gather in the grass and roses of this singing garden. The cradle in this orchard overlooks in its heights upon the heaven of Iraq's glorious future and humbly bows during its descent out of respect for this country's illustrious history. Meanwhile, the heritage of the garden's walls protects its pre-eternal heaven and eternal greenery. Not a single wrinkle in these walls, each of which contains a story from the pure ancestors, disappears from my dreams.

Under the auspicious care of visions, vicious animals, such as leopards, tigers or lions often invade my memories of the garden. It is as if their appearance one after the other is a creative production of the reality of war which transgressed against even the innocence of gardens and movements of cradles. How wondrous then is the garden of a house that appears in the purity of its origin in dreams while the violence of war puts on the mask of a predatory animal that did not have enough bashfulness to face innocence in body and still lacks it now in the realm of imagination.

The cradle also cuts the length of the garden with its eyes and alludes to its extension to the right, beyond the direction of human gazes. The beginning of the garden, under the cradle, as well as its end to the right and away from the gazes are ornamented with two necklaces of Raspberry trees. I can almost smell now these chandeliers as they gift us jewels without end and shake ecstatically when visited by relatives. As for the host of the garden, it is a cat that wanders in the courts of greenery and listens to the gossip of breezes as they shake the hands of grass.

The dust of the garden, in its embrace of the house's walls was like a perfect artistic portrait … between the heritage of the greenery and tradition of my grandfather's quarters is a window that plays the role of a mirror and molds a single meaning into two reflective senses and images. While this contemplative play is being held upon the stage of the house, the high walls of the courtyard are like guardians of a movie theater. They do not allow anyone to enter, except those whose inward and outward realities have been elevated to a station that exalts the honorable presence of culture and art.

The garden of the house which embraces the walls of my grandfather's quarters is not the only being with stories and conversations, but the abode in its entirety was the sultan of storytellers and dean of narrators in Baghdad. The ether of the place used to prepare itself every Thursday night for a larger gathering of relatives and loved ones who accompany the corners of the ancient palace in a journey of meetings and utterances. These visitors think they are the only living ones during these sojourns. They did not know that the features of the house were admitting the inclinations of breaths to memory after the dispersion of these assemblies and decades; like a historian who recounts an age that has gone extinct under the steps of learning and records.

The happiness of the house was apparent when the moment of these visits manifested ... You see the odors of foods and drinks race from the heart of the kitchen to the hearts of the family. My grandmother's Kebab with Tomatoes is a constant from the constants of goodness that was accustomed to the freezer's coldness and oven's heat. Its patience through these different temperatures has made it a symbol in my memory that represents an entire ministry of the ancestors' cooking. However, a group of advisors and consultants consisting of other traditional Iraqi delicacies assist this dish, including Spinach with Eggs, Rice with Fava Beans and Kahi.

I don't remember much from the legends of that house's second floor, except for my grandmother's room which overlooks through its window the garden and invites beforehand the precious necklace, my grandfather's cradle. However, there was another garden of a different type in the room's care. This second orchard hides in my grandmother's closet and also sends forth letters that contain the cologne of flowers specific to the room. As for the breezes, they remind of a sweetness perfumed with a state of generosity and kindness. As for the roses from which this smell emerges, it is precious chewing gum that my grandmother keeps locked like a hidden treasure. No one can see or taste it save children who have dressed themselves in the etiquettes of men.

Above this generous room there are other hidden quarters, if you were to wander in their paths and alleyways through the steps of the house, you would think you were on a very important climb in a hotel that has hosted all of human history in traditional Iraqi generosity. Your visit under the roof of the house ends upon the crown which overlooks the ancient footsteps of Karrada. When you leave the embrace of the house's interior to the eyes of its loftiness, you sense the emergence of the spirit from the prison of the body to the heaven of old knowledge, as old as time itself. The breezes that are contained by the organs of the house of traditional furniture and civilization harmonizes in perplexity with the neighborhood's birds that are carried by a new wind. However, it emerges from an ancient source with the same heritage and tradition as the house.

The face of morning used to flirt with the praises of night upon the gate of the roof. Each of them gives the other symbols and secrets which the onlooker enjoys as the revolving birds carry them to him. For each display on this roof, of night and day, there is a special ether and ornament. The glowing colors of morning spread with the perfume of the sounds of the neighborhood's alleyways and movements of merchantry. The life of the small hotel facing the house also gifts artistic portraits of Baghdadian existence.

The Two Wings of Tradition

If you look to the right, diving into the horizons of the neighborhood, within your eyes would dance the smiles of the sellers of Shawarma and desserts. Between the sweets and salt, the colors of Karrada are perfected also through the happiness of its residents and their difficulties. In the morning hours, the stalls and passersby attest to the gazes of heaven that bestow generosity upon the springs of sustenance for all Iraqis. At night, these stores also witness lights that remind one of Baghdadian gatherings and meetings that have been imprinted in the veins and streets of the city, just as it has been gathered between the walls of my grandparents' old house.

If your gazes were to turn left, your eyes would be delighted to see another vein from the veins of Baghdad, the stouthearted river of Dijla. The movements of this left wing of my grandparents' house harmonizes in its difference with the other wing which flies above the heart of the neighborhood. The alternations of buying and selling and histories of the

Baghdadians which they exchange across the pure breezes of their conversations, all of them are in an eternal marriage with the stories and legends of the land between two rivers. These overflow from the gentle whispers of the waters of Dijla to the passersby and then depart with their greetings and longing for the glorious ancestors.

The eyelids of the river are ornamented with eyelashes made of Palm Trees that allude, in their rhythmic harmony with the river's blue pupil, to traditional Arab beauty and also affirms the upstanding divine creativity that combines the beauty of the two eyes, body and spirit, in the essence of the one who's loved by the soil of this land. Its love for such a person melds in a reflection of the twin bodily and spiritual forms in the mirror of its heart's veins. For this reason, the whispers of this side of the neighborhood was, in its innocence, like a child that looks forward to a life it will experience for the first time. Meanwhile, the governor of the alleyways filled with stalls and stores was busy with waves of sounds from daily life: they made this governor, through their root and heritage, a grandfather for his river-brother on the other side of the neighborhood.

The river enjoys, night and day, the company of his family who ornament its eyelids with their humble short walks and manners of their nightly conversations. However, behind the curtain of innocence which the river wears as a costume, there is a majestic power that has accumulated over the ages that has transformed it into a teacher that can overpower the extinction of traces and a fortress that gives from its abundant goodness to those who embrace it from humanity. From the waves of this secret of Dijla overflows a visible influence upon the passersby. The springs of their speech became proper and correct through the overwhelming power of the river's purity. Just as the melodies of their brethren transmitted the vibrations of the alleyways and stalls … they also were the spring of sustenance and fountain of buying and selling.

Unfortunately, not even the river of Dijla, with the depth of its beauty and tradition, was able to obtain independence from the war's occupation and its effect upon the daily life of the water. Its lamentation, due to the fluctuation of the states of those who pass by, and the pain of their voices made it overflow from the inhalation of these turmoils upon the entire neighborhood. Amidst these events, the house of my grandparents was in its heritage the meeting place of the two seas of misery that crash upon its shores; one of them sundering forth from Dijla while the other invading from the alleyways and markets that have been filled with terror and lessons.

If your glass was to be steadfast upon the path of my mirrors, you would witness strings of days and papers of moments that throw aside the essence of eternity, happiness and homeliness whilst destroying the rosy cheeks of the walls of the ancestor's palace ... those walls that have become brittle in their age and wisdom. The sirens of war forced these walls, through their transgression, to exchange their age with a devastating calamity and remold its wisdom into a tale of its imminent demise. All of this was clear as the sun's heat when, one day, the door of the bathroom in the house screamed out of fear of a missile that overwhelmed the innocence of the neighborhood.

Notwithstanding these typhoons and storms of transgression, this house remained standing for mercy's sake and acknowledging the need of its family for comfort. It was able, through its heritage, to balance between perseverance and overflowing gentleness upon its residents at the same time. The consequences of such painful dancing forced the conscience of the ancient palace to perspire profusely in blood inwardly while giving in its stead a cold drink of tranquility outwardly. This is not surprising however, for this has always been the patience of civilization and tale of tradition.

Migration Within the Native Abode

After we moved from our house in Haifa street, we spent our last days in the Baghdad of love in this ancient palace of my grandparents. My transition was also from al-'A'ila (Family) to al-Hikma (Wisdom) schools in the neighborhood of Karrada. This in itself was a fluctuation that alludes to the reality of the affair and transformation of the country's utterances from the breeze of familial warmth to the dispersion of wisdom and destiny whose intentions were still hidden from all Iraqis at the time.

Like the rest of tangibles and sensualities in this journey, the change in the architectural atmosphere between these two schools was itself also a sad symbol of the demise of the manifestations of nightly conversations and expansion in the far regions of Iraq, with empty speeches of fiery transactions and constriction in its place. This meaning was embodied clearly in the shrinking of wisdom in between the walls of the narrow school; in comparison to the kind familial largesse firmly rooted in the court of the first school, in the now far Haifa street of bashfulness.

My experiences in these two schools also wore the necklaces of different states and dispositions. As soon as I entered the new school in Karrada, no trace remained in the breaths of my heart of the days of friendship and riding the school bus every morning in Haifa street. Indeed, my sudden coming was itself an intruder upon the symphony of friendship that was already established between the sects of students in the far corners of al-Hikma. All these incidents gathered within the confusion of my consciousness, which wandered between a longing for the past of stability and lamentation of the distance from independence.

After my father traveled to Jordan to find work and establish a new life for us, my mother and I tried to follow him during a trip in which the decrees of heavenly destinies were present. During those days, after the war, not a single flock of Iraqi airplanes flew above the skies to smell the Babylonian breeze nor even to convey the greetings of the Iraqi people to the corners of the earth. Rather, the fear of war tore apart the wings of adventure and planted in its stead a compulsory isolation.

Nevertheless, the crossings of war allowed for something of mercy to sneak in between its claws and overflow with an exhalation of movement upon the residents of Baghdad. However, instead of the birds of Iraqi Airlines from the distant past, travelers now did not find to ride after the war save buses that were, in the perplexity of their luxury and sluggish speed, like birds whose wings had been cut and were therefore forced to journey across the vastness of the desert in long days, which it used to traverse in hours that passed like the blinks of an eye.

This time, my mother and I rode the bus to Jordan. We cried fake tears that pretended to be in ecstasy about leaving home towards estrangement. These tears presumed that their imminent arrival, at that distance from familiarity, had become a certainty beyond questioning. As soon as the bus departed from the boundaries of Baghdad, the change in the atmosphere's colors alluded to the separation from lovers, including buildings and relatives. The desert of Iraq, made smooth with black rocks, was like a body struggling with loss of spirit. And so, it wore the dress of funerals, while its face was orphaned in yellow, due to the shock of the sudden calamity.

The bus continued its exit from the embrace of Iraq for a period that seemed to continue for eternity. The throngs of sleep used to wrestle with the boredom of wakefulness, in a march that descended into a typhoon of ambiguity. In those hours, the length of which had the patience of days, the passengers spent away all the conversations that resided in the emptiness of their beings. These exchanges, in their length and depth, were akin to descendants from the records of destinies. These travelers also indulged in feasts from all cultures, which they were able to contain entirely inside their luggage.

Moving from the bosom of Iraq to the other Arabian embrace passes through two stages. The first is a departure from a body with a certain nationality, while the second entails entry to another body, with another nationality; save that they share a single Arab patriotism that speaks in two dialects and longs for two lands and cultures. The snow of winter that gradually increased in appearance the closer we got to the Jordanian desert alluded to a peace secluded from the sickness of war. Although, the greenery of the military men's clothing who used to guard the extremities of home did not allow for even imagination to flirt with this peace…

The dispositions of these guards whilst they battled the courts of peace, was like a morning that confronts the darkness of night and opposes its coming … in an attempt that fails with an inevitable peaceful death. Indeed, that military greenery opposed our entry to the land of Jordan; and so, mercy forfeited my ability to see my father. The papers of government that decreed halting our entrance to the neighboring country, although revealing enmity outwardly, were declaring inwardly an honest longing from the motherly home of Iraq for a final embrace and kiss, before the realization of the burdens of farewell take their toll.

The hands of Iraq did not allow us to even see the neighbors' dust. Instead, its ancient perfume used all the greenery of the military to return us to its bosom. The drunkenness of the night appeared through the holes of the stern corners of the border crossing. The dark violence manifested as well in the corners of the place, which was empty of any joyous laity. Meanwhile, the subsistence of the army men was itself devoid of emotions. Even those birds with cut wings that had brought us to this desert port by land had departed with whatever was left of its energy ... it ran away from the death of feelings that was born through the mixture of dark nights and injustice of wars and their militaries.

This cup of emptiness and drink of nightliness warned of a possible transgression against a mother and her child, both of whom were breaths of the same country between whose fingers they now hang. The paralysis of the moment halted a bus in its tracks, as if it were sent from the gaze of heavens out of gentleness and mercy with those who were stuck in between the interstice of nationalities and no longer had an identity save the abysses of the desert and seeking the company of lost snow. It is as if this bus had come from the whispers of the unknown and contained wings of kindness that only seemed cut outwardly but hidden inwardly.

The heart, spirit and secret of this bird with hidden wings appeared in two men and one old woman from the Iraqi mothers. They were, in their mercy, like the very consciousness of Iraq. They laid, through the lights of the divine gazes, spreading forth the desert road which they crossed returning to Baghdad in a blink from the blinks of deep sleep. They did not have any conversations with us save the luggage of hearts which they effused upon us in comfort and tranquility ... These two sentiments returned us to my grandparents' house in the darkness of night ... as if we had never left that ancient palace or been separated from its immortal wings: the river of Dijla and noble alleyways of Karrada.

However, before the warm morning of Baghdad, busy alleyways of Karrada or journeying waters of Dijla could receive us, we were met instead with the face of my brother in that dim dark of night. In the features of his eyes was an astonishment at the moment. He was perplexed whether we had actually returned because our travel was murdered halfway or whether time itself had stopped and we were in front of my grandparents' house just as we were there that very morning. Either way, his eyes combined between a questioning and inspiration through which he tried to describe the fake justice of governments, wars and borders.

Next to my brother, my grandmother stood outside the house. She also had on her face the look of Iraqi astonishment. Although the queries of their faces, at that moment, were drowned in an ocean of our sadness for not being able to unite with my father in Jordan and our tiredness, that fed upon traveling endless distances in the desert. I witness now an artistic portrait full of anguish and feelings, wherein the colors of my brother and grandmother meet with the two men and old mother on the bus that delivered us home. For between the astonishment of the first group and tranquil generosity of the second, feelings are perfected under the brush that paints a story for the humanity of Iraq during the war.

The moments during which time stopped in the eyes of my brother and grandmother are harmonized with my father's eternal wait at the bus station in Amman, the capital of Jordan. I realize now that when I saw the shock in my brother's face, I also glimpsed therein a metaphor for the poem of my father's fear and worry. For he was put down by the delegations of humanness, within whose hands he put his hope to see his wife and son in another neighboring country wherein he now resided. A state that also drank from the cup of Arab pride.

Glimpses of an Iraqi Childhood

The memories currently deceive and lie in my mind, between the moment of our return to Baghdad and the next when we left it for the last time. These treacherous memories try to trick me with the excuse that I need to forget the tiredness and misery of war. It is as if those days had been drugged under a blanket of forgetfulness. Be that as it may, before I transition to that moment of final departure, I would like to, through the love of Baghdad the trustworthy, make of the breezes of the last of my memories an eternal and pure childhood, such that we can sojourn in its pathways, before we move towards the desert of old age and adulthood.

Nothing remains in the foundations of my Iraq save a throne from the many thrones of beauty and longing, under the care of my memories. The form of this throne is a kindergarten that faces our apartment in Haifa street, night and day. The name of this kindergarten harmonizes with the left wing of my grandmother's house, Dijla. Such a linguistic encounter between the epithet of the kindergarten of childhood in the modern neighborhood of Haifa and childhood of a noble river upon the banks of an antique neighborhood makes of Baghdad a fortress of perfected oneness … each of its organs calls for and embraces the other.

This is the reason why this mother of a country sends me now these letters that are like vines of linguistic eloquence; so that my last encounter with it in my imagination does not become a false claim of early aging emanating from the diaspora of war, but so that the mother country can stay laying down relaxed under the vast clear sky of childhood and its innocence, between the kindergarten of Dijla and the embrace of a river with the same name. Indeed, this is the sacrifice of a mother, she makes a river from the rivers of her veins a ransom for the consciousness of her child, they remain thereby infants who suckle from her heritage. Meanwhile, she remains aging upon the altar of safety for its infant's youthful past.

As children in this kindergarten that effused of innocence, we were like the liberated fish residing in the river of Dijla. Nothing occurred to our minds save the depths of the secrets of simple blessings, which we realized through our involuntary childishness. Right now, in the sense of smell that is firmly rooted in my memory, the odors of delicious foods consisting of white beans, which the Iraqis elevated to the rank of representing all species of beans ... these smells mix with the perfume of cleaning products that long kept the health of the place alive and well.

I do not remember the name of my teacher in the kindergarten of Dijla, but I know her gentle face very well; because it has been etched in my imagination with an ornamentation that represents the kindness of the Baghdadian face and femininity of all of Iraq. I also see a pathway, so detailed in its beauty and vast in its welcoming spirit that embraces a vast green courtyard. At the edges of this court lay many very tall apartment complexes that faced our house. Just as our apartment complex was proud with its beauty of Dutch construction, so was this other complex hugging the

Dijla kindergarten from the sweat of Germans hands. This is how the heritage of Palestine and modernity of the West met one another in Haifa street.

European Artistry, Baghdadian Auspices

I remember these German buildings very well, for we always used to visit friends of the family there, at the highest of the structures' loftiness. These friends have now been dispersed throughout the earth. Who amongst them knew that their apartments' identity concealed a trap of estrangement for them: "Just as we have been planted by familial hands in unfamiliar lands … you also will be embraced with this state of ours sooner or later!" And perhaps my memories wish to mock me now, because I remember during our regular visits to these friends that I used to watch the 1986 film "House" about a soldier who fought in the Vietnam war and after many years, ghosts of his friends, who died during the war, came back to seek justice from him for the rights of their memories…

Although these German apartments were smaller than their Dutch siblings, they compensated for this shortcoming in width with a height and loftiness that overwhelmed the first. They also espoused a different type of homeliness that squeezes its residents between

51

its embrace in an age of love. However, this small size did not stop the Baghdadian generosity from providing this apartment with eyes in the form of a veranda through which it would receive the breezes of Iraq and greetings of loved ones. Rather, it was easier for these apartments to fill its smaller organs with this air of tradition.

In the court of the noble and modern Haifa street compete other types of apartments that have been built by hands of workers from different ethnicities. They were in their presence in the court of our street like athletes who represent their countries in the Olympic competitions; each of them seeks to convey the professionalism and craftsmanship of his native land. Likewise, these abodes worked night and day to embrace all who see and live in it with the perfume of beauty, as the eye of architecture's spirit perceived it in the builders' country.

Nothing remains of these different architectural types save two that I remember now. My uncle's apartment was a courtyard with no end. This species of living quarters did not need hallways and wings to connect its' various parts. Rather, it was all one planet, within which were folded its handsomeness in an evolution of decorations that manifested spontaneously as soon as it meets the gaze of visiting witnesses. These differ with other kinds of apartments, owned by friends of my family, that were like a theater of colors, blues and reds, that meet all who invade its gates with a divan of a living room that gives the illusion that the house in its entirety is a throne from the thrones of the kings of previous epochs.

The Hospitality of Ghadir

On the other side of Baghdad, a city that has contained in its embrace the modern and ancient conversations of the past and released the future from the unknown, there resides the house of my aunt in the neighborhood of Ghadir, a stream that resembles in its age the banks of old Karrada. This house flirts, through its envious privacy, perfection and harmony of its organs the sea shell which houses inside a pearl hidden from jealous onlookers. Indeed, this house has not witnessed a single fault, neither in the sense of peace or beauty.

On the contrary, its garden that welcomes the visitor competes with the world's forests in its simplicity and decoration … Its grass harmonizes with its trees and flowers like a story that tells of the mercy the old have for the young and respect of the descendants for the ancestors. Beyond this, the house opens wide in welcome; not only from one door, but from two gates. Each of these represents one of the two veins of Iraq, Tigris and Euphrates … the river of the living room of tranquility and the kitchen, wherein the Baghdadian hospitality is planted and harvested in food and drink.

Upon this custom was completed the Iraqi generosity in my aunt's house. Our gatherings in this Baghdadian abode of memory was like a twin that resembles the nightly conversations in my grandparents' ancient castle upon the footsteps of Dijla. One living room could not contain the heart of the abode and spirits of its residents, which encompassed all tribes of relatives, friends and strangers under the care of its hospitality. Rather, it overflowed with these generous breaths upon another living room that used to embrace the first divan, which overlooked the eternal gardens … Meanwhile, the second divan had its special decoration of tradition and a supper table that attested for the generosity of the owner of the house across the decades.

For every room in this house, there are special memories that make the Baghdadian days living and fresh in my being. Such nightly conversations have also been cloned in the essence of every abode across the vast atoms of the country; each of them holds dear to memories from the past and memorializes its residents in spirits of imaginary forms that remain after the disappearance of bodies. Through the strength of the Iraqi tradition's perfume, if these memories are rejuvenated in the imagination of the one who calls them forth from their sleep, their new appearance is stronger than moments that had just disappeared a few blinks ago. Indeed, it is as if these memories had not died at all.

As for the second floor in this house, it contained between its folds a loftiness of conversations. These manifested in private talks between friends and relatives. Therefore, between the food desired by souls and weaved by Iraqi hands in the kitchen, living rooms that hosted all colors of families and the private quarters in the second floor, this abode of uncles and aunts combined between its shoulders a stage, upon which were performed stories from the life of Iraq.

The Christian Zephyrs of Baghdad

Elsewhere in Baghdad resides also the house of one of our family friends from the Iraqi Christians. Those who gave victory to their country with their love dressed as martyrdom. Their harmonious existence with the Jews and Muslims of Iraq had made from the strings of their land an emotional symphony. It weaves with the threads of its melodies divine litanies that advocate love for all religions. It also molded the land between the two rivers into a single spring for the oceans of prophetic laws and an eternal port for the singularity of the spirit, wherein all these different sects gathered upon the land of Iraq.

This kaleidoscope of the spirit dressed the humble abode with an ever flowing embrace between its corners. In return, the visitor could envelop the entire apartment with a single whirl from their gaze. It was a testimony to an ulterior dance of Iraqi generosity, unbeknownst to our vast palace in Haifa street or ancient fortress of my grandparents in the neighborhood of Karrada. Nay, it was a hospitality of nearness that melts into the beloved's own essence; a breeze of simplicity that is found at the root of all things.

What our exalted palace, built by the hands of Europeans, performed in ceremonious flashes of expansive halls, eternal cuisines and endless alleyways, this Christian monastery of an abode delivered in quick gestures that hastily transitioned the visitor between the enclave of the living room, dining table, kitchen and one of the endless gardens of Iraq; all on a red carpet of that familiar Baghdadian kindness.

Thus, the essence of this friendly home and our apartment is one, yet dressed as varying mirrors of colors that juxtapose under the spotlight of tradition upwards to blinding purity. This is how the engulfing Baghdadian breezes that surrounded the veranda of our apartment's kitchen conversed in the soundless language of hearts with the unrelenting greenery spread across the gazes of the dining room in our friends' home. It is as though the depths of the Mesopotamian soil met the Babylonian zephyrs for the first time, since ages immemorial, and decided to unveil their nightly conversations in love to two homes in Baghdad, wrapped in intimacy.

My memory serenades me now with gatherings that annihilate the contending forms of religion in august stygian Arabic soliloquys. The saintliness of Islam and Christianity married repeatedly into eternal bliss, and what was born thereof fathomed harmony in its entirety. It was a familial familiarity unawares of the fate of hate. Rather, like the elderly Iraqi date, it surrendered itself graciously as a chandelier on the open palm of divine gifts and grants; a heavenly tree whose ancient fruits foretold of the presence of Iraq in paradise itself.

This is how Baghdad kept the spark of love and its movement in incessant life. Across spectrums, neighborhoods and rivers, performances of cosmic dimensions reenact the eternal covenant between man and place, life and death and memory and nostalgia in a timeless play on a wandering stage with ephemeral actors. The ancient breezes' bequest is naught but the very will of divine decree manifest in the solemn temples of the Tigris and Euphrates, whilst they listen attentively to their passing guests on the riverbanks.

Such serendipitous relationships that carry the burdens of friends back and forth are what keep the memories of Iraq alive in my aging childhood. The dying forms of spacious palaces eroded by warring vibes, antique fortresses invaded by savage spirits and the other ghostly abodes lost between the spirit's stations all are quivering homages to recurring encores of a singular sacrifice of the body as it becomes a hum of death.

And so, Iraq bids me farewell now in the land of memory, just as it rested in peace from the agony of distance many decades ago. The only sigh left in this breath is but a simple halt at a restaurant, found at the threshold between Iraq and Jordan, wherein my mother and I tasted the Kebab of days gone by for one last time, before we transitioned into Jordan; a land with only a single river, but one vast enough to quench the entire thirst of my childhood.

Part III: Childhood Next Door
Across an Ocean of Sand

The last moments in Iraq lingered for what seemed like an eternity. The imminent separation between our souls and this native home paid homage to the inevitable death of bodies when they separate from heavenly spirits. Their veiled burial deep within the soil of the earth also manifested in an eventual interment of Baghdadian vibrancy within the lost alleyways of our memory. There, our senses kneel before the mercy of vision, and what the latter allows of images and forms to send forth from the smells and tastes of the distant past.

My brother inadvertently foreshadowed this nostalgic symphony with a somber bodily performance. As we lingered at my grandmother's house, ready with luggage that managed to carry the heaviness of farewells and estranged identities, my brother remained at the interstice of delayed departure. Perhaps he wished to circumambulate the streets of Baghdad, during this reminiscence of the prophetic farewell pilgrimage. Or, perhaps, he hoped to delay the inevitable, like an aging wave from the ocean as it thunders its way into the abyss of the sandy shore.

Alas, the invitation of that inevitable came coercively, and we undertook our own journey, riding a wave of tears across the sands of migration and diaspora. Suddenly, the scene at the bus station seemed familiar. For we were once again at the footsteps of decapitated birds from the Iraqi Airlines that were dressed like buses. This time, however, the imminent eminence of tears turned these buses into fragile boats ready to sail through the stormy ocean of sadness and fear of the unknown.

The gravity of certitude, this time, revealed the inexplicable versatility these spirits of transportation have, as they reveal the varying inroads of Iraqi crucifixion. Whether they embody the imprisonment of birds on the stage of the vast desert or perform a séance to the ravaging waterways of sadness in the theater of human separation, they inextricably honor the sanctity of art in redeeming the abyss of suffering itself.

And so, between our fazed bodies, butchered spirits and luggage mocking us between the leather covers of its contents, a literary artifact from my cousin synthesized all the actors and props of that moment into a climactic letter of farewell that was ornamented with physical relics that carry the sentence: "A tear of anger from me!" This pithy explanation directed the remnants of these relics into their proper resting places in my memory, as they await the moment when they'll be resurrected in abstract form.

These tears come back now, forgetful of their identity and lost in the amnesia of distant wars. It is precisely that ancient and inadvertent directive of passion: "A tear of anger from me!" which provides them and myself with a grant of harmony and conversation, under the auspices of nostalgia. A letter which lifted the tears of Iraq upon its shoulders, with more ardent difficulty than we carried the luggage of our identity, also performed, through the appropriate moment of its arrival, the very dance of the ocean as it sends waves of its children to the abyss of the sandy shore.

This letter also borrowed and killed the entire journey across the Iraqi desert from the very corners of my memory. Between the initial movements of the bus and my sister's anguished reading of the letter, which itself was embodied majestically by the ghostly apparitions of its author and other family members on the other side of the window, no images or forms remain of Iraq for the duration of this last treacherous hike. Rather, as this entire journey treads its way back into absent memory, it is overwhelmed by the joyful colors of union that await the separated organs of my family in Jordan.

So powerful was this deluge of novel movement and transition that Iraq survives only for a few more glimpses that sparked during a visit in 1994. My fleeting presence at the time in Karrada at my grandparents' castle leaves a final trace of familial happiness and friendly conversations; a fitting farewell for an abode that was eventually sold, after my grandparents passing, and bulldozed under the auspices of modernization. Thankfully, it survives more triumphantly now, in my memory.

A Neighbor with Mountains

My eyes perceived the unique identity of this neighbor next door with the sight of mountains. The flat solemn ground of Baghdad only knew of heights and valleys as a distant imagination in the northern ranges of Iraq. Of course, the city of two rivers nonetheless exquisitely performed these varying peaks in its masterful composition of a traditional symphony consisting of its peoples' emotions and passions through the highs and lows of everyday life.

And so, Iraq and Jordan convened in the realm of spirits in order to grant me a parting gift that immortalized my native abode in imagination. In this way, the tangible absence of these northern ranges of Iraq from my memory was redeemed by its reincarnation, within the endless slopes of Jordan, that met my gazes whichever direction my eyes whirled. This is also how these two brothers inculcated within me the essence of generosity and Arabian hospitality.

At the juncture of this masterful performance, I also emerged a son of a new fatherly abode, or rather, I was able to further quench my thirst from the spring of Arabism and better understand the contours of this transcendent identity. Between the geographic contrast in mountain ranges and linguistic sojourn in a vernacular kaleidoscope, I drank a wine of perplexity that fomented in the Gulf War and fermented during my childhood's nourishment in Jordan.

And yet, these mountains next door are the only traces in my memory from our journey across the ocean of sand. Like their physical outgrowths that ornament the surface of the earth, their apparitions now are *atlal*, artifacts, that decorate the moving desert of my imagination. They light the way forward, in an abyss of abstract nothingness, towards the colorful destination in Amman. Sometimes, I wonder whether this disappearance of the journey across the dunes from my memory is itself a performative act by divine providence that solemnly embodies the amnesia of the original moment; the fear of an unknown future and hollowed past that imprinted itself uniquely upon the canvas of my spirit.

For those elongated moments, that followed our movement across imaginary boundaries between two Arab countries, the illusory separation between myself, mother, brother and sister collapsed into a singular Arab identity that was destined to taste the darkness of diaspora incessantly for the entire course of modernity. In these moments that now escape my imagination, even the brutal greenery of military men and their rifles who guarded their imaginary boundaries has drowned under the hues of this performative act by the Arab identity and its journey towards the unknown.

And so, we traversed the imaginary boundary between Iraq and Jordan and yet my memory recollects nothing of the sorts. The imaginary contours of this separation between two wings of the Arab being is instead severed into colorless organs of non-existence. In the blink of an eye from the past, I find myself now in a moving bus that stops slowly at a station in Amman. A station for decapitated birds that resembles its cousin across the ocean of sand. Two stations that marry one another, under the auspices of an absent journey, into a powerful metaphorical portrayal of the *mahjar*: the home away from home.

The windows of the bus that delivered us to Amman was now drenched by pouring rain, another sensual homage to the tears of anger from my cousin's letter that betrayed the Iraqi sun which attempted to lessen the daunting inevitability of separation. The calligraphy of the 'tears of anger' also emerges as a flood of heavenly tears, while the blurry faces across the aisle of the window harmoniously reminisced of my aunts and uncles who stood in the same place, just across the ocean of sand.

Behind the blur caused by the heavenly tears, the familiar Iraqi face of my father emerged between the sad portraits on the window. Rushing out of the bus to embrace my bodily ancestry, for an ephemeral moment, the physical tears also embraced their heavenly counterpart and, together, they paid homage to the meanings of a tear on a cousin's letter.

A Safe Haven at the Peak of Tariq

My father led us to our first abode in Amman, Jordan in a sentimental parade that resembled, in its august spiritual state, the farewell caravan with which Baghdad delivered us into the caring hands of this Arab neighbor. It is through such divine providence that we were orphans of identity for only the duration of our journey, itself an absent and mutilated memory in the treasuries of our imagination.

We arrived at this new house in the darkest moments of the night. However, unlike the recent stygian visitors of Baghdad that hearkened for fear of the unknown, these serene breezes of colorlessness in Amman were anticipating an imminent serendipitous joy and, at the same time, paying homage to a trace of passing hospitality in the Baghdadian ambiance. Indeed, this the second, of many, honorable memories that Amman, the crown of Jordan, gifted me as a living emblem of the spirit of Iraq which gave birth to me and continues to sustain the notes of my soul.

This purity and sincerity of Amman's breezes flourished in our abode of color that resided on the mountain of Tariq. Even in those darkest moments of the night, the front door of this house greeted us to a conclave of furniture that hosted the spiritual essence of all colors. The brown hues of the walls, with the red shades of the furniture and glimpses of blues, that now compete in my memory for a precise vessel in the ghost of that abode, all appeared in such vividness that they triumphantly gave Iraq victory in my being. What had transpired in the war, at least during those first few moments in our abode atop the mountain of Tariq, passed into the deep slumber of defeat.

This moving tribute to Baghdad, with which every atom of Amman welcomed us, culminated in the conclave of spirits and presence of our new abode. Humbly, this fortress atop the mountain of Tariq did not taste the vast hallways or Parisian cuisines of our white palace in Baghdad; nor did it experience the aging wrinkles of my grandparents' castle of tradition in Karrada. Nevertheless, it combined between its hospitable walls a trace of lineage from each of these memorable abodes of Iraq. It was an immortal play taking place on the stage of Arab hospitality; the purpose of which was to make my first experience of migration seamless and seemly across the imaginary boundaries of the ocean of sand.

Perhaps this is why, like the performative act of forgetfulness which sundered any remnant of our journey across the sand into the custody of the ether, I no longer remember the histories of the kitchen or my room in this new abode. The hands of destiny decreed that, at least during the sojourn in the land of my memory, I should instead move through the hallways of this new abode and cross the silent distance to our primordial kitchen in Baghdad and my first bedroom in Haifa street.

All that remains of this new cuisine and resting quarters are ghostly apparitions whose spirits, usually consisting of the stories and contours of daily routines that color its life, now linger in the purgatory of a migrant's diaspora; they transition and fluctuate between the past of nostalgia's 'here' and false presence of its 'nowhere'.

And yet, amidst this serenade of ambivalence and confusion, the gift of Arabian hospitality flourishes and marries the memories of our apartment in Haifa street and abode atop the mountain of Tariq into a matrimony of spiritual union in the ecstatic being of one of their seekers, whose love for them is sustained by the distance of diaspora.

And so, the kitchen in this new abode surrendered the records of its cuisines lest they overwhelm the Parisian array of dishes from our white palace. And my new bedroom also relinquished the crown of its nightly soliloquys and friendly conclaves for those vast quarters overlooking Haifa street that were decorated with the ambiance of 80's musical life. Yet, with all these honorable tributes and selfless reflections of my native birthplace, this new home in Amman did not simply abdicate its throne in my memory. Rather, it still seeks to furnish its newly built imaginal castle with distinct furnishings of stories and meetings that quenched the thirst of my newly born and migrant childhood.

Overlooking Cliffs of Orchards

Our new abode atop the mountain of Tariq also compensated for its humble foundations with a captivating view that embraced its front gate; an endless valley that met, at its lowest point, the beyond of my imagination where the footsteps of Baghdad began. Here, also, I am able to collapse the prisons of time and space to convalesce with the Baghdadian breezes that once flowed through our kitchen's veranda on Haifa street.

The trees facing our house, on the other side of the road, shielded us from uncanny gazes that sought to invade our privacy and the boundless abyss of land that unabashedly tried to terrorize our serenity with the unknown. These trees, however, knew of this new migrant visitor in their midst and continued flowing the Jordanian ocean of generosity which had thus far carried us from the bus station to this new abode.

A movement of conventions among friends and riding my bicycle on this road, which was the mortar that cohesively danced in-between the bricks of our house and cliffs of orchards, now brings the surroundings of this new abode atop the mountain of Tariq to life. The thoroughly interweaved inroads extending east and west from our house form an intimate fellowship of veins that host the bloodline of the neighborhood, manifesting in the daily conversations between families and friends, on a red carpet of Jordanian hospitality.

Our house was but a single organ in this conclave atop the mountain. Its life now continues in dreams and visions that resemble the séances my sleep gifts as a tribute to my grandparents' house in Karrada. Unlike the savage animals of war that invade that aging castle of Baghdad, however, this harbor in Amman is ornamented by newer buildings and waves of souls that allude to the pre-eternal divine decrees governing the inevitable changes taking place in this world. These decorative alterations also effuse the perplexing life of nostalgia; how it thrives on distance and yet longs for its death.

This is how I journey with you in the various alleyways of this neighborhood, between its ornamented forms stored in my memory and embellished contours emanating from my imagination. The various sights to behold in the far reaches of the mountain now stand in my memory as planets around which the trajectory of our journey can pivot and traverse quickly beyond static forms into the subtle fluctuation of the inhabitants' states and emotions.

The local mosque of the neighborhood captivated the hearts of the people and their abodes with the timely prayers and religious chants that flowed from the minaret and mixed with the breezes that had just arrived from orchards up the cliffs. The short pleasant walk up the road from our house, which then meanders to the right towards this mosque performs now, in my imagination, the symbolic stature of the holy sanctuary in Mecca which resides in the easterly direction of my heart.

In return, the countless journeys I took back towards my house from this mosque hearken to the youthful wind of the east which brings, in its stead, the form of the beloved in glowing faith. It is here also that a white courtyard of marble, decorating the open and welcoming arms of the mosque, reminisces of its Iraqi cousin; that other white courtyard of marble upon which my younger self walked with school friends for brief moments that barely live now through the dense fog of a distant past in my memory.

Much like our house, and all other seemly homes in this mountainous conclave, the modest and pure white dress of marble and stone ornamenting the outer contours of this mosque's walls contrast beautifully with the colorful mosaic saturating the gazes of onlookers inside the prayer hall. These varying harmonious hues were not distracting the heavenly direction of the worshippers' hearts. Rather, they imprinted upon the gazes of their souls metaphorical glimpses of the essence of beauty and light, flowing forth from that realm of spirits beyond sensual images.

An extension of the giving spirit of the mosque can be found in a humble and cherished market on the outskirts of the sacred white courtyard of marble. The generosity of the store's owner, whose face embraces his forgotten name in my memory, also envelopes mundane incidents in the life of a child in elementary school. Whether it be the dire need for popsicle sticks for a school project or a sanctified desire for chips and soda for the nightly rituals of watching movies and playing video games with friends, this stall impeccably conveyed the unshakeable Jordanian hospitality we had become accustomed to.

I have traversed these vast veins of the neighborhood atop the mountain of Tariq several times in my distant physical past and on even more occasions that continue to thrive in my longing imagination and nostalgic dreams. Aside from the above mentioned visions that attest to an influx of novel souls and newly erected buildings, in other dreams still I tread the vast stretches of veins that connect our home to the other organs of the neighborhood. Traveling at the speed of love's light in these visions while crossing the roads, in paths that reminisce of the old physical ways we maneuvered from the outskirts to the center of our abode's heart, I relive an imaginal anticipation in my slumber that keeps the spirit of longing alive in my being, even during an awaken state.

Friends Under Mountainous Shades

If the conclave of our neighborhood was spiritually protected by Jordanian hospitality, then socially, it was thriving under the auspices of this Arab neighbor's military, whose ·housing complexes now hosted our migrant bodies. The overwhelming power of this spiritual talisman and detailed timeliness of its political body combined and manifested prudently in the endless valley ornamented by seemly orchards that guarded our house.

Under this perplexing patron, with twin faces of divine beauty and majesty, lived other souls that continue to play the symphony of this neighborhood's memory. The physical distance between our bodies, ravaged by migration, has not been able to murder the traces of these friendships entirely; they continue to linger and grow in embellishment in the crevices of the neighborhood and its meandering veins. This imaginal theater of everlasting relationships continuously resuscitates the persevering hope in igniting the spark of bodily encounters once again.

Next door, embracing the walls of our house, lived al-Hattab family, those who burn wood to ignite the fire of generosity in the desolate coldness of stygian Arabian desert nights. The face of Mu'taz, the al-Hattab's youngest son, still lingers in my memory as the first member of the family to ignite this flame of generosity, as he accompanied myself, my father and his, on the second day of our arrival in the vast *souk* atop the mountain of Tariq, just outside our conclave. The fire of this friend's kindness also stretches beyond the horizons of the mountain, for he was the first friend to accompany me across the endless mountainous terrain of Amman, from our neighborhood to the elementary school I was set to attend soon.

Unlike our house, which bore the imprint of a modern kaleidoscope of colors that serendipitously reminisced of our white palace in Haifa street, the al-Hattab's abode unabashedly proclaimed the traditional Jordanian hospitality found, at its best, in the humble tents of the Bedouin desert. Contrasting with the kaleidoscope of colors in our house, the calm grey and light blue hues in this neighbor's walls and tribal seating arrangement surrendered attracting the visitors' attention and instead directed their admiration towards the hosts; a humble aesthetic homage to that primordial Bedouin tent.

This subtle performance of modest hospitality and Bedouin generosity lingers now in my memory more than any conversation or event that took place in the al-Hattab residence. In itself, this is a testimony to the truthfulness of their selflessness, which mirrored its inhabitants' altruism. The walls' self-abnegating colors exalted the onlookers' admiration upwards to the heaven of the hosts' generosity, which now lingers humbly as comeliness with countless, yet forgotten, acts of generosity. In this doubly performance of selflessness, Mu'taz and the rest of his family also return the spirit of honor to these walls, as the latter stand now as paragons of that Bedouin hospitality in my memory's imagination.

The wings of our road stretch further beyond our house and al-Hattab's to also include the fluttering breezes of two Christian friends; both of whom transcended the effigies of time and space, in different ways, and overwhelmed language itself and my fresh wounds from the Iraqi past in a divine coincidence. Between the subsisting longing for the first and unrelenting presence of the second within the very spirit of the neighborhood's memory, it is clear that this Christian mantle of friendship was naught but an ambassador of ecumenical love, sent by the ancient Nazarene breezes of Iraq towards one of its migrant children.

The first of these friends is one characterized by the subsisting longing, from the Abu Hanna family. His first name, however, "Adi', also performed a linguistic dance that transcended the boundaries of time and space. For, inevitably, 'Adi was a constant reminder of the name of the leader's son of my native country, 'Udayy. Another generous performance by Iraq and Jordan that supplanted the tyranny of distant governments and instead placed a Christian friend with a familiar name in a ministerial station within my heart.

The cosmopolitan demeanor of the Abu Hanna family still colors my dreams of the neighborhood and strolls to their house. The retired military father had send his eldest son to Britain, and there this distant spring of the Abu Hanna family served as a thriving reminder of the dreamland just beyond the Mediterranean. As a witness to this vast familial network within which 'Adi was a captivating node, I glimpsed the first sparks of the Western spirit. My cultural dress of childhood in Jordan, weaved from the threads of 90's movies and video games that were produced across the globe in the New World, was manifest in 'Adi's embodiment of cosmopolitanism.

Just as our abode's ambiance brilliantly prepared for our arrival, as evident in the harmony of colors that remind the onlooker of the white palace in Haifa street, and the al-Hattab's residence humbly performed the traditional Jordanian hospitality of the desert Bedouins, so did the Abu Hanna fortress also recollect the ancient European castles of England whose aspiring admirers occupied the ether of the house with their vast demeanors from abroad.

'Adi's spirit runs through the life of my sojourn in Jordan and journey beyond, to the New World. Like the major signposts along the road of ephemeral breaths, our constant companionship atop the mountain of Tariq, and beyond the boundaries of that sanctuary, tethers itself to my memory as a generous gate to countless other orphaned images. It is his face, frozen in the innocent childhood of the 90's, that provides a sense of cohesion to that Jordanian life, which was suddenly lost and ended by coercive migration.

In this regard also, 'Adi's memory ignites the spark of life back in memories of countless hours with LEGO; the sacred ritual of play wherein a young imagination gives expression to meanings that reside within, through limited blocks, of varying shapes and forms, that simply exist, without. Here, once again, Iraq and Jordan carried the burden of an eternal act of kindness by allowing my enjoyment of LEGOs to migrate with me from the native homeland, without need for passports or visas; an act of generosity that tricked the savage obliviousness of the military guards at the borders.

The blanket of memories surrounding my time with LEGOs in Baghdad, in the cozy living room of my aunt in the neighborhood of Ghadir, contrast with the ambiance that gives color to these building blocks of imagination in Jordan. Atop the mountain of Tariq, 'Adi, myself and other friends situated these colorful expressions of our imagination within the breezes of the outdoors, under the gazes of the guardian orchards and cliffs. We sought to give form to nature's attempt of manifesting the divine infinitude by melding our fragile concoctions on the patient concrete surrounding the extremities of our homes.

These simple blocks of childhood now host us as I construct for you the countless images from my past, floating in the ocean of time. Like the other constants in the luggage of our migrant souls, that have serenaded us thus far and exhibited the collaborative spirit of hospitality between Iraq and Jordan, these German toys have also been granted safe passage, by these twin Arab countries, from war to peace in pieces; a noble effort on their part to allow me the grace of reconstructing the remnants of my childhood in friendly paces, atop a mountainous conclave surrounded by orchards and cliffs.

The memory of my friendship with 'Adi is also ornamented by a certain delicacy for virtual arts which I began indulging during the early days of my arrival in Jordan. Video games still color my appreciation for culture as a vessel for divine manifestations; and now it's a thread of spiritual movements that intimately marries my past to present. If 'Adi's cosmopolitan soul in my memory helps revive the traces of my childhood in Jordan, then video games are the candle that illuminate the darkness of forgotten images and forms in my countless conversations with this Christian confidante.

My progressing journey with video games, an ascension into the heaven of sophisticated artistry, from the abstract Picasso-like style of ATARI to primordial life forms in the first PlayStation, mirrors my eclectic travel from childhood to maturity. This is how ATARI, PlayStation and 'Adi's Game Gear eloquently reflect a certain simplicity and breezes of liberation that characterized our Jordanian childhood. This contrasts with the sophisticated realism which moves within the current digital apparitions of today and reflects the dress of responsibilities and delimited rationality that governs our every movement as adults.

Like the myths of old, my friendship with 'Adi had an imaginary third wing through which the original moments of our companionship soared through and still survive in the vast ocean of imagination. Film, the ancestral form of virtual arts, also presents itself as a shore of creativity, which I have treaded throughout my life in search for meanings that elude the strictures of language. Nay, often, they were treasures that spoke to me while I was completely unaware of their very existence. Film regularly ignites sparks of unbeknownst dreams and visions; flames with reiterating colors unknown beforehand to the cosmos.

Like video games, film has also established itself as a signpost to greet visitors who tread the path down my Jordanian memories. The war-torn vestiges of my Iraqi days are highlighted by a repeated indulgence in James Cameron's *Terminator 2: Judgment Day*, a rather foretelling performance of the imminent future of Iraq at the time. As Linda Hamilton says at the end of the movie, "The unknown future rolls toward us. I face it, for the first time, with a sense of hope. Because if a machine, a Terminator, can learn the value of human life, maybe we can too." In many ways, I had carried these words with a sense of hope until the present moment.

And yet, for all the apocalyptic zephyrs which Cameron's masterpiece unleashed in the span of two hours, it remains today much more merciful than the war that physically divorced my Arab body from the spirit of its *watan*, native country. Unlike the warplanes that invaded the vibrancy of our white palace in Haifa street, the Terminator, as Linda Hamilton expresses, knows the value of this human life and now serenades my being with gatherings at my aunt's house in Ghadir where Cameron's masterpiece played on the antique television. It recounts the performance continuously, all the while capturing images of the attendees who will one day be resurrected in my memory through the window of this film.

As this movie continued to live in my heart, as a vein to the early years in Iraq, my arrival in Jordan is decorated with new art forms from this genre; ones that ostensibly mark my first breaths in this neighboring land. Two specific films act as figurative wings that facilitated my cultural landing in this new Arab society and, like the *Terminator*, also eloquently performed the ambiance of my existence at the time. As I write this, the cartoon *Aladdin* and Tim Burton's *Edward Scissorhands* unleash countless waves of memories that storm past my spirit's eye to permeate a network of other motions and utterances in the vast reaches of Amman; all together, they revolve around my infatuation with these two films.

Like ATARI, these two art forms were the first artifacts I owned, itself a rare luxury for a migrant in diaspora.

In retrospect, owning these two video cassettes, themselves immortalizations of an artist's creative act, in a sense eternalized, embodied and internalized a refugee's ability to own, at the least, their own memories; to metaphorize belongings, accrued while in relentless movement across time, space and imaginary boundaries, as stable anchors in the political ocean of diaspora. Perhaps this is possible only through art; for it is itself a refugee of creativity without boundaries, and so it craves to provide hope for those who have been torn through the suffering of distance and may only find redemption by longing for an impossible act of return.

Edward Scissorhands, an eloquent snapshot of Tim Burton's distinct artisanship, intimated my diasporic status as a semi-foreigner in a new society. The distinct Iraqi dialect that colored my tongue with heavy syllable and consonant pronunciation followed in the footsteps of Edward's distinct extremities that stood out among all the other perfected human hands in 'suburbia'. The danger residing in these metal hands of Edward also emanated within the foreign estrangement inherent in my Iraqi alteration of Arabic.

Meanwhile, Burton's unique gothic style of heavy burdens of black and grey colors were a constant reminder of my *watan*, native Iraq, in its new war torn dress which the custodian of the two rivers wore in a funeral procession, lamenting the deceased vibrancy of Baghdadian breezes and a glorious past. In this way, as a migrant in diaspora, alongside countless others, I sacrificed my individual identity as a worthy cause for the wounded primordial abode. We not only performed the Baghdadian malaise, but also attracted its energy as it permeated sparks of creativity across oceans and seas, as it did in Burton's work.

On the other hand, Disney's *Aladdin* tried to alleviate this diasporic separation by mocking that distant ocean of sand. It is clear to me now that this cartoon was an impeccable embodiment of the Arab proverb: "The severity of a calamity is what makes me laugh!" While many perhaps found the portrayal of Arabs in this film to be a stereotype of savagery and backwardness; my gaze was drawn incessantly to the cartoon, because I knew that the tyranny back home really did "cut off your ear if they don't like your face" ... it's barbaric, but hey its home!

Facing this artistic reflective mirror, I was in a position of power, akin to what Steven Spielberg described in one of his speeches, that through his movies, he was able to externalize his fears and share them with a larger audience. I also faced demons from a not so distant past and place; but I did not desire, in this case, to imitate the native tyranny by conquering or invading its cartoonish ego. Rather, Disney's flamboyant extravagance of that ocean of desert arrived to my senses as a gentle joke from that native land and a reminder of its inhabitants' indelible sense of humor, with which they were able to declaw the goliath of all calamities simply through an overwhelming deluge of mockery and humor.

In this way, I was able to sunder *Aladdin* such that it was no longer Disney's production, but an emanation from my own soul. Vibrating strings of resonating sound flowed through my conscience even beyond the first few moments of the cartoon wherein the desert visitor describes the horrific conditions 'back home'. I also found homage in the symphony of 'riff raff, street rat' to the migrant despondency, and the hopeful red carpet parade awaiting their arrival at any home … here, or away from home.

As I write this now, I'm also reminded of ethereal moments that obsessively sing the memory of another masterpiece by Tim Burton, the original 1989 Batman. I recognize, after involuntarily unearthing this imaginal artifact from my past, that this film was my first encounter with the director. Between these two poles of gothic artistry, serenaded by blacks and greys, I find it quite fitting that my diaspora and separation from Iraq is taking place within this Burtonian interstice. Here also, a masterful performance by Jack Nicholson, as the Joker, presents me with the mockery of war and savage animals that have invaded my dreams of Baghdad. I decipher in between the lines of this artistic destiny my task, as Batman, to face such demons; dressed in the very darkness of my soul's abyss. Nay!

Facing that very abyss to discover the light of redemption through forgiveness.

Only such a repentance with a blinding glowing flame can extinguish the tyranny of a Joker. To subsume the unmitigated chaos of life within one's realm of responsibility, I'm convinced, is the route to tour darkness within the healing circumambulation of light. Perhaps this is why divine providence ordained that my recurring viewings of Batman in Baghdad took place at a theater that was serendipitously situated in a vast garden. The contrasting demons of Batman's confrontation with the Joker were alleviated by this greenery of Baghdad. Likewise, the darkness of my separation from this native country remain under the gaze of a vast green dome of divine grace.

This is how movies and video games have allowed me to turn my friendship with 'Adi into a timeless parade, taking place alongside Baghdadian events and places foreign to its Jordanian spirit. This should not at all be surprising, since the ornament of constancy emanating from Burton's imagination is a sibling of our listening act at the *atlal*, traces of colors and contours of tangibility residing in my memory and distant childhood. Hopefully, it has become clear by now that my journey with you is not an obsession over departed souls and their countless nuanced conversations. Rather, my desire is to convey to you how the landmarks of my past still stand today in an imaginal embellishment. They are resiliently living, not through the auxiliary role of supporting props, but rather impeccable witnesses to the utterances of life.

And so, we return to 'Adi's cosmopolitan home atop the mountain of Tariq and the revolving artifacts of art that have facilitated immortalizing those years of physical proximity in memory. Towards the end of my sojourn in Jordan, 'Adi inadvertently prepared me for my forthcoming journey to the New World by taking me to the American embassy in Amman, where we watched *Around the World in Eighty Days*, in a crowd of ostensibly foreign faces from across the ocean. Under the hospitable auspices of their embassy, they were finally home during those moments. Meanwhile, I was still the migrant stranger, even though I was still on Arab soil.

The aura of cosmopolitanism emanating from the Abu Hanna residence sends us further down the road to the second Christian abode. The friend residing in this second landmark imprinted his throne in my memory through an act of embodiment altogether different from 'Adi's hospitable treasuries of cosmopolitanism, films and video games. Instead, this friend encompassed within the boundaries of his name the entire ambiance of the neighborhood, Tariq. This is all that remains of his apparition, a name which he carried triumphantly as he hosted a new migrant friend on a tour in the veins of a mountain which carried his name.

Tariq's house was a simple one, or at least that is how it veils itself currently in my memory. Undoubtedly, it is following in the footsteps of the other abodes mentioned thus far in this neighborhood; homes that have honored the personalities of their owners and immortalized them perfectly, whether in colorfulness, traditional Bedouin hospitality or cosmopolitanism.

Likewise, Tariq's home also presents itself as a mirror reflecting my friend's passing apparition in my imagination. Aside from the name imprisoning this property in place, nothing remains of its vibrancy and distinction among its sibling houses in that street.

I do remember attending Tariq's birthday party, surrounded by his many sisters and parents. I recall feeling apprehensive because his family's festive inclinations declared that all attendees had to participate in group, charade-like, games. As the ceremonious festivities proceeded, a moment of awkward silence screamed as I was put on the spot to participate in these competitions, which I refused. As the many sisters stared at me, their faces remain frozen in that form until now. Defying this unintentional paralysis of the spirit is Tariq's only other movement across the earth of my memories: a trajectory connecting the neighborhood to our school, Deir al-Latin, the Latin Monastery, in the Northern Hashemite district of Amman.

This is the same spring of education that hosted myself, Mu'taz al-Hattab and this Christian friend who embodies the neighborhood's name in my conscience. As we transition now to that school's vestiges, we maintain a gaze towards this neighborhood atop the mountain of Tariq. Indeed, my daily life at Deir al-Latin reveals the school's marriage to our homely conclave in more than one way. Most importantly, as a Christian monastery of education, Deir al-Latin soars in a wind of universal tolerance that emerged early on in my life, in the humble abode of Christian friends in Baghdad. Here, however, in the Amman of Bedouin hospitality, Deir al-Latin signaled my growth in Jordan, from childhood to maturity, exclusively at the hands of monks and priests.

A Hashemite Latin Monastery

Buses were the only portals available to take us from our abodes to school in Jordan. Like the decapitated birds that painfully transported us across the ocean of sand from Iraq, these yellow siblings also treaded the roads in patience. However, unlike their distant relatives, they carried us in a serenity that redeemed the earlier suffering of diaspora.

Save for various moments of arriving at the gate of Deir al-Latin, in the northern Hashemite district of Amman, and stepping off the steps of the bus, I have no recollection of these yellow vehicles picking me up from my house atop the mountain of Tariq. This peculiar amnesia, like a forgotten dream, that has erased the journey of time and space from the mountain peaks and valleys of Amman has eloquently molded these yellow school buses into time machines that intimately folded the physical dimensions of geography and moments within the embrace of my imagination.

The spacious veins of our neighborhood atop the mountain of Tariq, ornamented with pure white brick houses that shared the same textured fences, contrast with the ancient narrow streets of this northern Hashemite district that harmoniously hosted an antique monastery in its geographical center and spiritual heart. However, by token of its contrast with the simple modernity of the neighborhood atop the mountain of Tariq, this old district instead resembled Karrada, in the heart of Baghdad. This second wing, alongside the river Dijla, to the bird of my grandparents aging castle finds now a perfect symbiotic overlap with this Christian monastery in the Hashemite district of Amman.

As my grandparents' castle, with its familial records of nightly conversations, convalesces in a sentimental projection upon the Deir al-Latin monastery, the old alleyways of Karrada, and first wing of the family castle, also converse with the sibling stalls and restaurants hosting Arabian hospitality, of the Jordanian flavor, to the passersby. Meanwhile, the mercy of imagination decrees that the absence of Dijla from this Hashemite district requires a creative substitution under the auspices of divine grace. Here, the long stretches of roads and vast barren land connecting our neighborhood atop the mountain of Tariq to this monastery and aging district marry the memory of Dijla and its purpose in Karrada.

In the boundless dry horizons embracing these pathways, upon which the school bus is inevitably concealed as a time machine, one finds an impeccable homage to the limitless generosity of Dijla and the its eternal perseverance as it listened and recorded the incessant conversations of visitors. Likewise, these vast stretches of roads foreshadowed the highways of the New World as they listened and immortalized the gossip of travelers who were transitioning between two distinct worlds; like a soul traveling through the *barzakh* of purgatory, from the realm of bodies to spirits.

This liminality granted these roads power, especially in the case of a journey like this, through the maze of my memory. The true nature of this power is metaphorical and another instance of a harmonious overlap across moments and places. Like Dijla and these highways away from the New World, we also stand at the interstice of distinct places and their unique textures with varying ages. We are traversing a barren absence and erecting connections between these disparate artifacts in order to construct a narrative of harmony and sense in a world filled with senseless diaspora. In other words, like Dijla and these vast roads, we are also engaging in a séance to a present moment destined for an embellished past.

Most importantly, through the lens of divine grace, this is, yet again, one of many instances in which the spirit of Jordanian hospitality convened with the forgotten Iraqi conscience in order to provide a displaced migrant with a solemn cure, in the form of a harmonizing creativity with enough power to displace the trauma of war with an orphancy of non-existence and imaginatively return the despondent souls to their native springs.

The ancient walls of the monastery and surrounding street also performed this dance of similarity with my grandparents' castle and Karrada neighborhood. In my imagination, this effect of aging on the school's countenance, facing the street, has now melded perfectly with the adjacent buildings. In turn, such blurring artistry allows for the monastery's contours to extend across the entire bodily outline of the district, whereby the entire northern Hashemite hemisphere is rendered a sacred conclave for monks.

Like the mosque and neighboring market, which ornamented the center of our neighborhood atop the mountain of Tariq and transformed the heavenly chants into worldly gifts, this Christian monastery in the Hashemite district also extended a meaningful hand of generosity, in the form of a small stall wherein a kind middle aged man sold us falafel sandwiches that have withstood the test of time.

Walking through the spacious gates of the monastery now further augments the antique ambiance of European castles that had filled the ether of my grandparents' home in Karrada. There is a subtle nuance of aesthetics that overwhelms such old places. For example, the untrained spiritual eye may suppose these aging walls, when veiled by a rusty metal door with steadfast bars that lack the serenity of curvature, to be foreboding claws of an ancient prison. Whereas, in reality, they are an architectural embodiment of the cosmic elderly hand, embracing and protecting.

This paternal shelter also manifests in a brief glooming shadow that harbors the main gate's archway, just prior to opening a vast courtyard that symbiotically completed the arch's metaphorical mission by manifesting an inner, limitless kindness of the cosmic elder. And yet, like the proverbial virgin on her wedding night, the heart of the monastery, wherefrom the spring of tutelage gushed forth, was located deeper still in the spatial abyss of age.

As a fading memory, there is a large enigmatic niche, possibly more, hiding within this initial welcoming courtyard. Fortunately, the dark ether of its ambiguity is contained now. Like a dormant tumor, it shows no signs of attempting to invade the other aged yet thriving hallways and rooms of the monastery residing in my conscience. In the movie *Inception*, it was stated that a sign of dreams is that one cannot remember when and how they begin. In a sense, this ambivalent alcove in the facial features of the monastery marks its current image in my mind as an imaginal bastion and passing trace of its former self.

Just as monks in the monasteries of old ascended in the heavenly spheres of knowledge by descending deeper into the abysses of self-realization, we the students of Deir al-Latin also took some preliminary steps down large stairs at the other end of this welcoming courtyard. The culmination of this architectural performance of one's plunge into the soul was met by various rooms where learning and celestial ascent took place. Moreover, in an impeccable homage to the ancient monasteries, these halls of learnings formed a central, large spine that provided balance for the entire school on the edges of time and space.

Here, the monastery of education dedicates another act of honor, this time towards the mosque atop the mountain of Tariq. The homage taking place in this center of the school, however, was writ large and at large for all of Islam. It was a poignant communique, unveiled only for creative gazes, between two faiths born and reared in this region of the world. Christianity and Islam spoke to me those countless decades ago, and only now the taste of their monologue ferments in my imagination, after it had fomented through separation and longing.

This honorable act appears in the pivotal position of the halls of learning, as a spine, around which the entire heart of the monastery pivots. Surrounding this large structure of rooms is a walkway that completely encloses it; rendering it a desired island of learning that is surrounded by the streaming waters and waves of students. Like the very Ka'ba, residing at the center of Mecca and occupying the throne of Islam, this spatial focus of the monastery's learning also attracted the gazes of seekers who circumambulated its circumference in their daily journeys, from the secular peripheries of the outer walls to the inner sacred sanctum of spiritual realization; filling the very ether of the building's brick and mortar with nostalgic eternal life.

The movement of this circumambulation flowed like gentle blood in the veins of the monastery. This is how this Christian school also performed a dance of resemblance with our neighborhood atop the mountain of Tariq. There, as here, the walkways of pedestrians and vehicles served as arteries and veins that connect various organs of life in harmony. At Deir al-Latin, the veins of circumambulation fulfilled the covenant of cohesion between the shrine of learning and spine of tutelage, in the center, with the wedded virgin and heart of the monastery, which resided beyond the gazes of onlookers.

At these footsteps of the circumambulation's natural demise, began the ascent to self-realization on the humble shoulders of Jordanian Christianity. The towering floors, that seemed to extend endlessly at the bottom of the steps, embody for me now a magical

Arabian phoenix whose wings are open in a timeless embrace surrounding the spine and shrine of learning between the wind of its flutters. These incessant breezes flowed from the ancient rhythm of learning that emanated from the classrooms located on the left wing and reverberated back from the right wing. Meanwhile, this latter extremity is represented by the pure greenery of trees that are as antiquated as the monastery's walls and entire district's age.

This metaphorical eminence of the towering heart of the monastery finds succor in a daily routine which took place in the earliest hours of the morning and ignited sparks for limitless ascensions that reverberated in all the atoms of the school. This was a sacred ritual whose sanctimonious timeliness projected the spiritual ascensions of the students, into the heavens of self-realization, upon the very imaginal phoenix of the building; all soared in the enchanting confluence of Jordanian, Arab and Christian heritage.

This daily collective prayer, for a secular age, was the mandatory salute of reverence to the Jordanian flag; to be experienced and tasted in a military-like composure. Like the countless ethnicities that converged upon the *Ka'ba*, unified by the monotheism of their devotion, this sacred ritual of the secular age returned the favor by uniting the waves of religions under the auspicious gaze of the *watan*. It transcended the confining boundaries of bodily laws by erecting a mystical *Ka'ba* of self-realization as a shrine and spine of a Christian monastery.

The eternal testimony to this universal inversion of ancient faith is its resurrection and emergence in the imaginal conscience of an Iraqi Muslim migrant, like myself, whose love for Deir al-Latin was reared in a Jordanian childhood and nourished entirely by Christ's followers. Perhaps, then, this confluence of the oceans of Islam and Christianity, at the shore of Arabism, is the homage which my memory would like to gift this Abrahamic cousin on a red carpet of creativity.

Like many of the other human traces emerging in this Souk, the sensual traces of friendships and relationships are vague in Deir al-Latin. Instead, all I remember is the ambiance which I share with you here. In a similar fashion to the sites which mark our neighborhood atop the mountain of Tariq, there are a few classrooms in the monastery that emerge as august stars around which the entire building's imaginal galaxy revolves now. These are the sacristies where I'm certain I have spent countless days at the school.

The divine hands of grace strategically placed me in those locations at the time, such that now they serve as instances of those critical organs of the monastery, around which its entire imaginal life thrives. Moreover, the varying color schemes that ornamented each of these halls, mostly ranging between browns and greys, fluctuate between the perplexing mixture of distinct experiences, which they allude to, and unified antiquity visible in the wrinkles that marked the hues' textures.

And so, both Mu'taz and Tariq, my two friendly traces from the mountain of Tariq who studied with me at Deir al-Latin, are now dressed in colors that match the halls and courtyards of the monastery; a harmony of dyes set in motion by the events that tethered these people to those spaces. In the presence of such a powerful visceral elixir, the utterances of rational books and records of misunderstood school assignments dissipate into oblivion at the hands of an orchestra playing a symphony of direct taste for the senses.

There is one more site that marks this monastery as living in my memory; one that augments the sensual appreciation for such a life. It is a small stall that resided hidden behind the embrace of the spine and shrine of the school. In the very corner of the monastery, this small market was simultaneously closer to the entrance facing the Hashemite district, yet at the very end of a visitor's journey, through soulful descent and spiritual ascent, across the contours of the school. The spatial positioning of this stall, underneath the welcoming courtyard which opened the monastery's arms to the outside, was a riveting symbol of Christ's humility that ornamented the Jordanian hospitality emanating from the school as a whole.

If the countless classrooms and halls of learning performed the dance of spiritual ascent through their flowing chants that reverberated between the wings of the school's phoenix, then this stall played a mesmerizing melody embodying the selflessness of a perfected and disciplined saintly soul. The dark hallway facing the stall stretched like an expected tunnel to the afterlife; here, also, it foreshadowed a silhouette of the stairs marking the beginning of one's life in this monastery. In between the gloomy warmth of this eternal corridor one also sensed the selflessness gushing forth from within the monks of old; an altruism hidden and buried … unknown even to the welcoming courtyard above.

Like the peaceful heart of a saint, which gathers the longing souls of devotees to its nexus, this stall also attracted the journeying students from across the vast corners of the monastery to its dark abyss. There, they were gifted material food commemorating the Eucharist in its depth and joy. This is how a simple bag of potato chips can linger for decades in the memory and conscience of my lips. Its physical body died but was resurrected endlessly through an eternal Christic breath.

My time at Deir al-Latin in the northern Hashemite district was a short lived sojourn, not in its end but the dream-like suddenness of its beginning. For I started studying there during second grade, whereas Mu'taz, Tariq and the countless other students had tasted the ether of Jordanian monasticism there for a few more years beforehand. Thenceforth, after graduating from third grade, some local migrations transitioned me across the waves of Amman's ocean; all within the auspices of this Arab country that kept my diaspora contained between its embrace, for now.

From Tariq to a Prophetic Mountain

Our first home in Amman, atop the mountain of Tariq, was married to my education at the monastery of the northern Hashemite district. Sometime later, beyond the scope of my memory's strength at this moment, my family and I left this safe harbor overlooking cliffs and orchards and we migrated, within the hospitable contours of Amman, to another home; an apartment atop another generous mountain in this capital of Jordan.

The mount of Husayn prepared to host us for a couple more years in a sojourn that was not destined to last in the warmth of this neighboring Arab embrace. From peak to peak, Amman performed its impeccable kindness to migrants in the most holistic spirit possible. I'm not seduced now by this city's apparent submission to the hands of divine grace that moved my family and I across these prominent landmarks. Rather, I'm bewildered by the that soil's pure disposition which attracted such a divine gaze of care towards distant relatives.

The breezes of life that moved the neighborhood atop the mountain of Tariq differed in mode and style from their counterparts in the vicinity surrounding this new Jordanian highland. The spacious roads of the veins that caressed the orchards and cliffs facing our home in the first peak reflected, through these contrasting mystical shades, the divinely ordained calligraphy consisting of narrow and busy streets surrounding our new apartment.

The addition of this new abode to the curriculum vitae of our migrant identities also molded new metaphors, similes and assemblages of resemblances between the various homes, neighborhoods and countries that had carried our burdens through the years. Much like the eclectic and disparate portrait which harmonized between the color schemes of our house atop the mountain of Tariq and spacious palace in Haifa street, this new apartment in the mountain of Husayn also married into the existing relationship between our two previous abodes.

The corporeal form of this new home resembled in its genus, as an organ in an apartment building, our white palace in Haifa street; just as our first Jordanian residence, atop the mountain of Tariq, was a self-standing villa and younger sibling of my grandparents' castle in the heart of Karrada. While this temporal sequence of spatial forms inverted the history of our migration within the Baghdadian embraces, the internal spirits of our sojourns atop the two peaks in Amman followed their Baghdadian counterparts harmoniously.

This latter performance was evident in the contemporary colors of our first place which, as we have stated beforehand, resembled in its modern elegance the vibrancy of that white palace in Haifa street. On the other hand, the aging walls of solemn greys in the second apartment on the shoulders of Husayn reminisced of the ancestors' fortress, between the wings of Dijla and busy streets of Karrada. The distance between the internal spirits of this latter and first abode intimated the similarity between these same esoteric aspects such that, in many ways, our new apartment atop the mountain of Husayn, was a tranquil homage to my grandparents' harbor of tradition.

Beyond this shore, just as a single Christian friend in our neighborhood of Tariq was enough to embody the namesake of the entire mountain which carried the veins of the community upon its shoulders, the name of this new highland, Husayn, sufficiently collapsed the distance in time and space between the heart of Karrada and this equally hustling and bustling quarter of Amman. The suffering of Iraqis through the centuries and quibble of the recent war turned into a redemption, through the unrelenting perseverance of the prophetic grandson Husayn. This neighborhood, across an ocean of sand, also paid homage to a descendant of that crucified Husayn. A king for Jordan, whose dominion and love, residing in the hearts of all Jordanians, represented a metaphorical symphony of the inner victory of his first ancestor.

Between the breezes of this prophetic lineage flowed the intimate harmony of my grandparents' castle in Karrada and our new apartment in Amman. In return, the surrounding environment atop the mountain of Husayn also obliged to this undergirding spiritual harmony. The palm trees of Baghdad that veiled the virginal beauty of Iraqi dates at every street and alleyway find a mirroring reflection here within families of trees that filled the streets of the mountains in an ocean of greenery.

In comparison to the young custodians of the neighborhood atop the mountain of Tariq, my young friends Mu'taz, 'Adi and Tariq, our landlords at this new premises were an elderly couple, whose first names have now been forgotten and sacrificed for a mere parental appellation that better harmonizes with the spiritual metaphor governing the memory of this entire neighborhood. Abu 'Isam and Umm 'Isam were two senior Christians embodying the ancient traditions of Jordan.

The *'isma*, infallibility, of their ancient souls sundered them mere hospitable markers of their travelling son, 'Isam; just as my grandparents rendered themselves ministries of Baghdadian dishes and drinks for their converging descendants every Thursday evening. Amidst this soliloquy between distant ancestors and the Christian narrative governing our residence, and my education in Jordan, which found its spring in long lost Iraqi days, this new apartment atop the mountain of Husayn was a testimony to a universal consciousness directing the diasporic movement of an immigrant family in modernity.

The inner organs of our new apartment also revealed a simultaneous change and hearkening to styles of hospitality and tradition. In contrast to the villa atop the mountain of Tariq which poignantly declared its generosity in a kaleidoscope of colors, this new abode compensated for its varying shades of a singular, solemn grey with a sudden vastness and immediacy of stations that overwhelm the hidden quarters of the residence facing cliffs and orchards. In this regard, this new apartment further inclined to the age of Baghdad, as it combined the spaciousness of the white palace in Haifa street and ancient openness of the castle in Karrada.

For one reason or another, the aura of this new residence had left its traces, in a special way, within the vast land of my imagination; in the twin forms of vivid dreams and memories. Both vestiges allude to the records of significant events that had taken place under the auspices of this apartment of tradition atop the mountain of Husayn. This is how this abode performed the secret theophany moving within the spirit of homeliness: the wisdom that they themselves are treasuries of imagination and allusions to related events and people that have converged upon the furniture, rooms and halls of such residences.

All the while, such quarters stand as records that withstand the erosion of time. As hosts and landlords thrive and perish, humble objects seem to linger through the obliviousness of their presence within gazes, both during the lifetime of people and then to the great beyond. They slowly capture the sequence of forms emanating from the spirits of their owners, culminating with the inevitable demise of these human souls and their complete imaginal migration to the tombs of these memorabilia; a diaspora and exodus that intimates the bodily transition under the soil and spiritual movement upwards.

And so, as the human body and spirit harmoniously meld with the breezes that ascend and descend, spirits of objects spiral horizontally and dissipate into the ether of *khayal*, imagination. This is how and why this apartment atop the mountain of Husayn continues to live, as an extra spirit, in my being. A vivid resurgence of certain facial features of the ambiance ignites the spark of an event that is ordained a familial relative of this apartment's history. In reality, this entire journey into my past has been a narrative of objects, while people have remained props born of the former's story.

The first twin, a vivid memory, appears now divorced of its historical temporality. Instead, its tale has become a timeless spatial arrangement of this residence in my heart. Nevertheless, a solitary indication of moments emerges for this twin, in the form of a deep stygian night. As I lay on my bed, facing the large window that gazes upon me, the light of a full moon shines down from just beyond the life of the window, above the house. That same full moon that has carried the countenance of desires throughout history also illuminated the ambiance of that night, which in turn immortalized the fragrance of its image in my memory.

Next to my bed, I had put a cassette recorder on low volume so that the singing emanating from within can rhyme completely with the silence of the night. The song playing on the recorder belonged to the Egyptian singer 'Amr Diab, called *Habibi Ya Nur-l-'Ayn*. The pomp and circumstance of this production had just seen the light of day when this memory took place. As 'Amr Diab's latest hit was serenading every street and corner of Jordan and the Arab world, it also left its traces in my apartment, bedroom and calm nights. Perhaps, this common artistic thread is what married the fluctuations of life in Amman, at the time, within the confines of this singular night, in my room and our apartment to the serendipitous occasion of this moment; all through the humble auspices of an extinct artifact such as that cassette player.

The hospitality of 'Amr Diab, as he sang about his 'beloved, light of the eyes!' manifests itself in the very events governing my life at the time, within which this vivid memory dances impeccably. At some other corner of Amman, I recognize a distant dying memory, taking place just hours before the movement of the stygian night in this memory, whence our family attended a party where this song was playing. I remember this not only because of the song's spirit which lingered across both occasions, but also the sweat across my forehead, then and there, which attested to the hustle and bustle during the earlier hours of the evening.

I also recognize now that as I lay in my bed, I felt the weight of those traces, from a near past, across my forehead and melodiously in my ears. At that moment, in the serenity of the stygian night and under its magnanimous care, I tasted the first genuine experience of resurrecting the past in a corporeal effigy of creativity, all within the boundaries of my imagination. As the comfort of my bed facilitated my physical gaze into the unknown nightly space and veiled luminous moon, my inner gaze also traversed the abyssal night within and explored the moving pieces of an event that, just a few hours beforehand, had been a bastion of immovable physicality.

The other twin, of vivid dreams, sends me forth from nowhere to an eclectic mixture of roads and pavilions that resemble the main street which guarded the long private road, at the end of which our apartment sat as a mount in the corner; a highland embodying the mountain upon whose shoulders it rests. In these visions, I find myself maneuvering through these moving imaginal pieces of a tribute to the past, reaching the crown at the heart of the private street.

The ability to simply reach the footsteps of this ancient apartment usually accomplishes the objective of these dreams. I never go inside to traverse the staircases and find our old apartment within. How could I? Migration had sundered it a forgotten secret, sealed and concealed within the abysses of diaspora and time. The only permissible premises available for visitation now, in the vast land of dreams and visions, are these outer courtyards and streets. Most importantly, a gentle arbor governing the archway of the apartment building, between the private street and staircase, lingers in my dreams as the closest effigy to the private concealed quarters.

This is hardly a coincidence, for this rhyming hymn of the past in the imaginal realm is an inverted foreshadowing of a forthcoming future that spreads the red carpet to the current awakened present, whence I'm spending my solemn adult life in the city of Ann Arbor. Just as this gentle arbor softly rescinds invitations to re-enter the apartment of old age, so does it annihilate queries into divine destiny which decreed that an arch of nature, of all things, is what foretells of a permanent life across oceans of water and culture.

Turning around, brokenhearted, from the stairs to the concealed treasure, I march in my dreams to the meeting place between the arbor and private street. In these visions, this road becomes a sea port that returns me inevitably to a life of exile. To make sure this march to the shore of ambivalent identities takes place in a timely fashion is a police station residing to the immediate right of our apartment building, at the very end of the private street.

Like our apartment building, this station of law enforcement also stands as a nebulous interior with foreboding exterior. The primary distinguishing mark of its formlessness, however, is that it finds its frivolous shapeless origin during my physical residence in this apartment in the mid 90's. Like Edward's haunting castle overlooking suburbia, this police station simply lingered during the years of our sojourn atop the mountain of Husayn. The influx of police officers treading inwardly and outwardly from the heart of its quarters gave me no reason to engage their proceedings meaningfully.

All the while, little did I know, this unintentional ambivalence on my part was preparing this architectural object for the primary role of instigating a haunting ambivalence in my memory. The serendipitous coincidence of its presence as a guardian bastion at the head of the street also allows it to subsume and better embody the imaginal role of overseeing those deafening marches, across the private sea port, to the life of exile.

Returning to the inner contours of the apartment that are welcomingly open in the conscience of the first imaginal twin, in contrast to the second, various quarters await our portrayal in order to receive the permanent imprint of actualization, away from the confusion of potentiality. My aforementioned bedroom lay in the far northeastern corner of the apartment, situated beyond the spacious living and guest rooms, both of which embraced one another in divine union.

As for the *harem* of privacy, which included my bedroom, beyond the hospitable soil of the apartment, it consists of a stretch of rooms that converse with one another in a soliloquy of endless familial gossip. The Baghdadian memory of Babylonian breezes which left its traces in this apartment saw that all three private quarters should be granted a window overlooking boundless skies and a greenery guarded by a comforting wall that surrounded the building from all sides, save the entry point from the arbor.

The sibling of my bedroom, alongside these other quarters of the *harem* kinship, was the kitchen, which also enveloped the living and guest rooms; albeit from the opposite side of my private room. Together, my space of isolation and kitchen gazed upon the twin alcoves for family and guests. Together, my bedroom and kitchen received the sustenance of hospitality from two oceans, these objects of gazes and windows that permitted the Arabian breezes to reside within the perimeter of our house without passports or visas.

Meanwhile, as an Arab migrating under the mercy of such documents, I was given two extra folds of sustenance, beyond the share of the liberated rooms, in our Jordanian apartment. I also tasted the unique delicacy of Iraqi food in diaspora, mixed with the creative feelings of Ammanian breezes that sought to languish the anguish for distant Baghdadian zephyrs. The second, more subtle, share emerges now, in spatial and temporal separation, from this home away from home wherein loose imaginal forms of old stern objects move freely in my memory like the very independent breezes which serenaded these objects' surfaces decades ago, and which allow them now to remain living during our journey in this story.

Like our first kitchen in Jordan, atop the mountain of Tariq, this ancient homage to Karrada atop the mountain of Husayn was just that ... a vestige. It performed in its reduced size the inevitable dream-like state of diaspora and constriction; especially in comparison to the long lost Parisian cuisines on Haifa street or traditional ministries of food in my grandparents' castle. Instead, these new cooking quarters sought to constantly remind us of the current separation from a native home and imminent possibility of continuing departures.

And yet, it managed to compensate for this treachery of the age using the same tool: homage to tradition. It is here and now that you might, as I do often, feel bewildered by these living vessels for migrants in neighboring countries and how they combine between reminders of the lingering pains of instability and unbounded welcoming hands of generosity. More so than that, how they perform both these painful and curing acts through precisely the same medium: a constant and incessant deluge of memories from the distant native home.

Among many others, I could say that this *hayra*, perplexity, is precisely what sustains our residence in this *hayr*, safe harbor, of migration and diaspora. It is a contending mixture of safety and anxiety that, as stated elsewhere, can only ferment into an intoxicating soothing wine for the senses once it is allowed to foment for many epochs in the deep tombs of the heart and its throne, the vast ocean of imagination. At the time of my physical sojourn in these Iraqi and Jordanian abodes, I merely enjoyed the innocent taste of a visceral childhood.

It was an anesthesia which had sundered my body and being a porous record book for those moments, whence now I'm revisiting places from across the ocean turned into timeless frames in my life. It was a necessary sedation that precluded me from contemplating the possibility of leaving my second home, Jordan, abruptly; a scenario which would have single handedly invaded and murdered the vibrancy of my surroundings in that new land, much like the war systematically terrorized the ancient spirit moving through our Iraqi bedrooms, kitchens and verandas.

Ultimately, that is how the hands of destiny leave their imprint upon our lives, through weaving an elixir of sedation and unawareness in the very atoms of our daily breaths. Thenceforth, we are left chasing the nostalgia of a past, residing just a few blinks ago, and a present we are unable to perceive in its true state: as a kaleidoscope of moving imaginal waves traversing an ocean of spirits and meanings.

And so, at the end of this tour of our second Jordanian abode, atop the mountain of Husayn, I find myself resurrected, again and again, towards the imprinted memory of 'Amr Diab's song, 'beloved, light of the eyes', which thoroughly stirs that precious night under the full-mooned window of my bedroom into a

Jordanian rendition of Don McLean's *Vincent*, a timeless cultural artifact commemorating an immortal artistic emblem of the heavenly spheres, all through the brush of suffering and strokes of redemption.

A Metropolis for a Neighborhood

My regular outings with friends atop the mountain of Tariq in the spacious and clear veins of the neighborhood, afar from the hustle and bustle of the main street, contrast with the immersive location of our new apartment atop the mountain of Husayn, in a metropolis of markets and exchanging glances of capitalism that filled the nearby streets with incessant economic life; one that made itself known in the very breezes that came into our apartment.

Here, yet again, is a reminiscent tribute to my grandparents' castle in Karrada. Akin to the wing of human interactions which allowed the ancestor's abode to fly in the sky of Baghdad, alongside the other wing of Dijla, the busy streets atop the mountain of Husayn, ornamented by countless stores of an infinite variety, also helped our new apartment to soar atop a peak of prophetic lineage and a Hashemite legacy.

My countless traverses across the main street connecting our apartment to the main artery of the mountain's neighborhood harmonizes now with the infinite flutters of both wings of tradition, there in Amman and beyond any place, in the distant and forgotten effigy of Karrada. However, the generosity of this ongoing hall of mirrors and similarities refuses to allow this new apartment to construct threads of harmony with my grandparents' house in exclusion to the other residences slumbering in my memory and imagination.

Therefore, a few other streams of imaginal silk now weave themselves in a river like Dijla from this apartment, across the rivers of time and place, to both the neighborhood atop the mountain of Tariq and our white castle in Haifa street. From the first abode, our new apartment borrowed the metaphor of landmarks as essential signposts to keep the memory of the neighborhood and entire mountain living and thriving to this serendipitous moment in the present.

Meanwhile, from our farther blink in the past, my first home in Haifa street, this new apartment re-established a bus-stop for school, which converged upon the meeting place of the main street with the private road that concluded with the jewel of the police station guarding our apartment building. This halting station for our old friends, the decapitated birds of transportation, play two essential roles on the stage of my memory: both as a thread of friendship with Haifa street and a node of partnership with the neighborhood atop the mountain of Tariq; this is understandable since such marked obtrusions in the geography of childhood are themselves landmarks that make locales eternally living in memory.

And so, this new neighborhood on the hospitable shoulders of Husayn performed the generosity of its prophetic namesake by extending the already infinite web of parallels and imaginal projections between these endless neighborhoods in my memory. As I continue to explore this past, in writing, with you, the countless frames of this movie also continue to synthesize themselves into a personalized mesh of *tawhid*. A transcendent monotheism beyond form, tasted through a never-ending procession of forms.

As if this generosity of metaphor was not enough, this new prophetic neighborhood extends its hospitality and makes the image of the bus-stop even more vivid. It accomplishes this by helping recount the presence of a peculiar scene across the street from this station. There, beyond a streaming river of relentless cars that are a difficult obstacle for crossing pedestrians, resides an illegal convergence point for taxi drivers. Unlike the solemn march of the decapitated bird of transportation that took me to school every day, these miniature modes of movement sporadically and chaotically clashed upon the pavement. In their unseemly hasty arrival and sudden departure from the side of the road, they were like a force of nature collapsing upon its prey, just prior to fleeing from a bigger predator seeking their demise.

And indeed, the prey and predator of these taxi drivers is not merely an imaginal projection for a physical non-existence. Rather, the hired workers were attracted to the absence of police officers. In turn, the ominous suddenness of the law enforcement's appearance sent them fleeing away from this illegal stop, which was –

ironically – just across the street from its legal sibling. I wonder now, if the divine memory of the police station guarding our apartment had decreed such a coincidence in the proceedings of my life, for the sake of that overflowing spring of similarities and parables.

Further down the road, to the left and nearer to the heart of the neighborhood, lay the other landmarks of the mountain of Husayn that resurrect the neighborhood continuously in my conscience. There is truly no comparison to the endless main street which connected our private road to the busy marketplace down the spanning wing of the mountain; for the neighborhood atop the mountain of Tariq was shielded from such endlessness by the cozy comfort of the cliffs and their orchards.

The first site that beholds visitors in my memory is an archetypal vestige ornamenting and directing the dance of hospitality in this part of Amman: a small all-purpose market, just on the corner of the private road which sustained the endless feasts taking place at our apartment with God's nourishment grown on that land's soil. Now, also, the proximity of this stall to our apartment serenades my imagination with a metaphorical semblance between this abode, the monastery of Deir al-Latin and mosque atop the mountain of Tariq, all of which shared the distinguishing feature of such a mercantile breeze.

The street which housed this market, and stood parallel to the private road to our apartment as twin streams of livelihood running through the neighborhood, also contained a historical spring of memories ornamenting my stay in this neighborhood. There, I experienced the Korean martial art form of Tae-Kwon-Do for the first time in my life. The subtle contours of my engagement with the fighting arts is itself a landmark that requires a solemn sojourn at each recurring instant of its commemoration during this journey, beginning with its initiatory phase taking place here atop the mountain of Husayn.

The exact reasons why I decided to enroll in this center escape me now. Like many of the incidents, events, movements and people in my life, this dojo has also compromised the abundance and details of its human interactions for a more subtle spirit animating its residence in the imaginal realm. It no longer stands as an end in the story of my childhood, but rather one of countless metaphors that extend the images and forms of my earliest years beyond the boundary of a single wave, to an ocean of waves capturing the entire childhood of life.

From this imaginal conglomerate emerges now a possible reason for my initial interest in martial arts: to tell a story of diaspora and redeem its suffering by mastering an artistic bodily dance of rigid contention. I am able to present myself, and yourself, with this mythical reason only now, after decades of reflections that allow such an understanding. However, at the time, I was under the same anesthetic that numbed the frights of diaspora and migration under the overwhelming joy of a simple childhood. It was this pure primordiality, mixed with my subconscious mythology, that eventually drove me away from the martial arts center.

The rigid conformity of the center's practitioners to the form of Tae-Kwon-Do, and their neglect of its universalizing spirit, subconsciously contended with my mythological desire. The trainers choreographed endless competitions between students, while I sought a singular monologue with the ongoing diaspora invading my identity. It was only this epic struggle which piqued my anguish's interests and trampled any motivations to perform its mimesis in the sparring of human bodies.

We linger with this mythological thought until some later time and continue traversing the landmarks of the main street connecting our abode to the heart of the mountain of Husayn. Beyond entire schools of architecture that manifested their prowess in houses and buildings, lay a modern relic in the heart of this antique neighborhood. It was an intentional aesthetic statement, intended to reflect the inherent spirit of technology moving within the building. This was a computer store which holds an insurmountable importance for my sojourn in this neighborhood.

Just as the humble market sustained our kitchen with endless feasts, this glamorous store also left its imprint upon our apartment in the form of the first computer my family ever owned. This was the second step in a long journey with technology, beginning with the celebrated ATARI atop the mountain of Tariq, that continues to shape my imaginal understanding of the present moment and creative engagement with a dancing past.

Further down the road, the curvature of the pavement hinted towards the imminent arrival of the busy stores hugging their adjacent siblings; one after the other to an endless horizon. Between the mark of this modern computer store and beginning of the marketplace are hazy forms and images of initiatory and sporadic restaurants and stores that prepare the visitors' sights for the incoming transgression against the calmness and serenity of the residential quarters.

I believe this haziness is an intentional performance by my imagination, in order to preserve a certain reverence for the more essential sight guarding the beginning of the marketplace: a regular pilgrimage site serenading my childhood's proclivities to the hidden mythology of video games. This was the al-Aqsa store that sold these forms of virtual interactive culture. This shop fills my childhood with its energy that permeates all my later engagements with video games, including my current spiritual nourishment through this art form.

This store patiently recorded the first six years of my engagement with video games, throughout my sojourn in Jordan. My earlier initiation in ATARI prepared me for a secondary ritual whereby I experienced the contours of Super Nintendo. Here, also, I would like to pause for a moment of reflection over my soul's taste in the games of this machine, at the time, and how they reflect a spiritual symbiosis with the metaphors of Tae-Kwon-Do and martial arts.

Like many others my age, I became attracted to many of the newly released games during this period of the 90's. My fascination and ritual observation of cartoons like *Aladdin* and the *Lion King* was coupled with a proclivity to forge my own story in the gaming renditions of these movies. Alongside these regular indulgences, however, I was also drawn to other iconic releases at the time: Mortal Kombat, Doom and Street Fighter.

I vividly remember these interests causing tumultuous conversations with my father who regarded the first two games specifically as ornamenting my mental state with unnecessary gore and violence. Interestingly, I do not remember my attachment to these games pertaining to any sense of gore or blood, but rather a fascination with an ordered and systemic triumph against obstacles that culminate in a progression to the final destination.

It is somewhat clear to me now that, like martial arts, fighting and horror video games were a way to channel an unfinished personal story to its climactic end. Perhaps it was the ghost of the war that had returned to refresh its wounds and was met by an enduring spirit of childhood that sought to settle the affair of liberty once and for all. Or, perhaps it is my subconscious desire to overcome the inevitable distance from Iraq, coupled with the perplexing need for my nostalgia to continue through this separation that altogether manifested in virtual mythology.

Whatever the reason may be, Mortal Kombat and Doom is now imprinted in my narrative as a vivid representation of struggle and a dance of tensions. As I sought with pain to obtain these games, against the opposition of my father, I also remember attempting to find a sweet solitude among some of my friends in school who had been given the permission of fate to play these games. And yet, I am also met now with the perplexing question of how the crave for these virtual myths expressed itself at the time, in my subconscious?

Indeed, this is an essential query since emotions are married eternally to nostalgia, even the particular flavor of which animates my life story here. At times, I almost hear the old childish desires again revisiting me, if only to allow me to glimpse what they felt like at the time. However, what words can describe such ancient aging meanings? What sounds or voices have the power to give life to memories that have become part of death itself? The only thing that remains of this mix between life and annihilation are the vestiges of vivid colors, shapes and characters that have now lost their luster.

Ultimately, this is the only way I can describe the hold which these games had over me at the time. The procession of pixels that translated into life, thanks to the power of electricity, through my hands seemed like a coordinate dance of ancient shamans who sought to whirl me away from the physical world to pseudo-physical spaces and enclaves. At times, I seemed to sacrifice the smooth realism of my life in Jordan for these pixelated gifts from the New World, all for the sake of the ability to ephemerally wear the garment of virtual powers to maneuver through my distanced and nostalgic identity.

Perhaps, also, this is why this new neighborhood of Husayn provided me with an entire maze of arcade machines wherein I was able to exercise my negotiations with a warful past through exorcising a traitorous distance from home. Even though this *mujamma* (meeting place) did not serenade visitors with renditions of Mortal Kombat, they still provided a worthy substitute under the name of Street Fighter. Thousands of kids, my age and older, converged upon these arcade machines like an endless stream of time travelers ready to step into liminal canvases wherein they could participate in an artistic production from the West.

What exact awareness did these members of my generation of a Jordanian nationality have of the subtle American stamp coloring the spirit of these games? I'm not entirely sure. However, this is a question I ask myself often now, as I was … like them at the time, constantly rendering these interactive myths as an inseparable component of my own Iraqi, Egyptian and now Jordanian identity. We did not refer to the characters in those games as American audiences did, and if we did, we intentionally butchered the pronunciation. How wondrous is it that now I'm an ocean of space and time apart from Jordan, living in the New World from whose bosom these virtual myths continue to migrate elsewhere! Yet, I'm also now craving that Old World which remains young in the ocean of my heart's memories.

A Second Hashemite Monastery

The transition of residences across mountains also carried with it a migration from one school to another. Like the kinship in geography which harmonized my previous and current abodes atop mountain peaks, divine providence also brought together my tutelage under the singular banner of Deir al-Latin, albeit under the auspices of different forms. The Christian hospitality which first hosted my immigrant soul in the Hashemite neighborhood now welcomes me to the same school in a more modern wing of Amman known as Tlaa' al-'Ali.

Like the Hashemite origins of this monastery, this neighborhood also conjures infinite memories that collide into a nostalgic mix within the finite confines of my longing heart. My imagination roams more freely and vividly in this modern sector of the city than in the ancient Hashemite quarters. Most probably, the length of time which we I spent in this school, spanning the entirety of my fourth to sixth grade education, coincidentally overlapped with my maturing mind, in

155

contrast to the shorter two years overwhelmed by the anxiety of a child who recently arrived from a war-ridden homeland.

I would like to begin with the school itself, this branch of Deir Latin, and then expand outwardly to the neighboring veins and streets. In this way, this monastery, a younger version of its Hashemite sibling, can emerge as the heart Tlaaʿ al-ʿAli. Indeed, this is a status which the school deserves, if for no other reason than its geographical performance of this centripetal attraction which witnessed its residence atop a hill that branched from Gardens St., the main artery of the neighborhood.

Like its older Hashemite brother, this younger and more vibrant monastery also hid its courtyards of knowledge behind a wall that surrounded the corner of the hill. In this regard, the age difference between the architectural siblings emerges in subtle directions of humility shown by the Hashemite elder that are not as visible here. Whereas the aging walls of the first branch melded and melted with the surrounding ambiance of ancient streets and stalls, here the guards of bricks surrounding the hilltop maintained a distance from the nearby sights and sounds. In both its elevation and distinction, Deir al-Latin Tlaa' al-'Ali was like any young life filled with the zeal of exploration, indulging the advice of old age briefly and with swift courage.

This younger sibling also displayed its youthful extravagance by propelling its courtyard of white marble immediately behind the protective walls, undoing the layers of bashfulness which had veiled the walkways of circumambulation of the Hashemite monastery. Instead, the one and only vast heart of this jewel in Tlaa' al-'Ali was immediately accessible to visitors, merely beyond the entrance that connected the inner sanctum of learning to the vein of the hill. Long gone were the guardian trees and descendant stairs that set apart the conclaves of learning within a separate dimension, under the guise of architectural illusions. Here, the voices of students and their bickering preceded the lessons and classes as a frontier of the pride of a youthful generation.

Perhaps, it is this youthful extravagance that has granted a bigger imprint to Deir al-Latin Tlaa' al-'Ali in my imagination and memory. The mere sound of uttering the school's name, and the neighborhood's, is enough to unchain a deluge of nostalgic memories that comes rushing down my imagination straight to my heart, whereupon I dive to try and decipher the whereabouts of old friends whose fazed faces now smile at me namelessly.

These partially dissipated friendships are prime examples why this journey of mine with you concerns places and textures and not people and events. For truly, I rarely remember conversations and incidents. Rather, my being sought since that past's inception to obsess over the surrounding environments that hosted these ethereal meetings. And so, now I am left in the perplexing conundrum of contemplating the fragile nature of human interactions. Had I known, 20 years ago, that I would forget the names and voices of my best friends, would I have taken greater care to immortalize them?

Incidentally, or perhaps not so much, most of these friendly apparitions emerge from acquaintances I have met and made during my years of study at this branch of Deir al-Latin. What remains of most of these ghosts is a first name and body, both of which are in need of a last name to tether them to the technologies of today and databases wherein I can find them. I have discovered this unfortunate reckoning after hours of searching on social media for these lost souls. The end result of these queries were a series of recent pictures of the school that has merely increased my longing as it illusively erected a present-day image of my childhood, while compromising its aging grain in my imagination.

There are the brothers, Ma'an and his younger sibling whom I have completely forgotten his name unintentionally. It is an ever mysterious irony of destiny that I would forget the name of the brother who was closer and dearer to my heart. And yet, their smiling faces serenade me with a breeze of imagination now that grants me enough perseverance to enjoy their company in the privacy of my memories and hope that our beings will meet again someday in this physical world.

And then there are two friends with a singular name, Fadi. One of whom was a leader of sorts among the students and the other was a pale skinned boy who remained somewhat aloof from such a leadership position. Alongside the first, celebrated, Fadi is his competition for fame and leadership, Yazid, or perhaps Ziyad. The cliques that surrounded both these figures now appear in my imagination like hazy spirits that dance around the central, and only, courtyard of Deir al-Latin Tlaaʿ al-ʿAli. It is a funeral procession for my past and memories.

I could never overstate the nostalgic force that emanates from this school. It has confidently become a vortex that allows me to travel swiftly to the past and linger there in a timeless hospitality. Often, my preoccupation with these friends who are now in history's 'lost and found' has overwhelmed my usual inclination to immortalize textures and places. Nevertheless, it is the necessary homage to the walls of this school, between whose embrace I met these friends, that we now direct our attention and imaginal devotion.

Much like its older sibling, Deir al-Latin Tlaa' al-'Ali hosted the daily morning ceremonies, during which students, teachers and all the atoms greeted the Jordanian flag in religious love, in the central courtyard. In the case of this younger building, however, this routine communal breath was much closer to the public eye. It was as if this branch of the Jordanian monastery sought to reveal its heartbeats to the public, whereas its older sibling wore layers of veils made from ancient concrete and privatized sanctuaries. Although I have sundered this contrast as a contention between an elder's humility and experience and its younger kin's brazen embrace of life, I would also like to think that these two branches of Deir al-Latin complement one another's mystical attempts to manifest the monastery's Christian ideals: lingering between the Divine Hiddenness and Worldliness, Singularity and Multiplicity.

Like the older sibling's courtyard, this younger and smaller Deir al-Latin also extended the wings of its courtyard in various directions, some that went up the stairs into isolated classrooms while others ushered forth large foreboding buildings that housed countless classrooms, administrative offices and prayer alcoves for devoted priests that managed the affairs of the school in Christ-like humility. This courtyard also has its shares of fabled and faded spaces that remain now only in their ghostly shell, much like my lost friends. Like these migrant souls, these architectural niches are also missing many of their previous limbs, save for a first name and shape … perhaps.

The front gate to the school was met, at the far opposite corner with the stairs to the isolate classrooms. My memory also seems to reminisce over a little planting area used to train our young generation, at the time, to love the last traces of a thriving greenery. It also foretold of the irony embodied by impeccable care given to a few plants in the middle of cities and careless destruction hurled at the large mass of earth's organic spirit. Alas, in those days, we did not contemplate these deep thoughts. Nevertheless, Divine Providence had ordained that such pithy epithets would emerge eventually in a different time and place.

One of these classrooms reminds me now of an incident hosted between its walls. A scuffle between two students, who happened to be my friends, continued its performance during class hours. Unlike the private and reserved demeanor of teachers in America, a motherly Jordanian English teacher attempted to instill the love emanating from Arab hospitality between these two pupils.

On the opposite side of these familial conversations lingered most of the classrooms of Deir al-Latin Tlaa' al-'Ali, all of which were also secluded behind walls of privacy that reminisced of the virginal sanctity of the courtyard of this school's older sibling in the Hashemite district. My memory manipulates my emotions as it holds back any recollection of the exact number of floors which the main building contained. Either way, I only remember the highest floor, most endearing to heavens, and recollect sitting in its educational convents.

It was there that my first day of classes at this school took place. Like many of the ambiguous names of my friends and hidden identity of floors, the exact occurrences of these inaugural days also elude me now. The only thing I remember is a brief moment during which one peer, Fadi, decided to single me out, the immigrant kid amidst a sea of Jordanian children; a performance to which, as my memory serves me now, caused me to roll my eyes in embarrassment.

There are a few, very concrete, other memories which Fadi hosts in my imagination. I remember a brief scuffle with him once at the end of the school day during which he pushed me and I acquiesced without a response. Although this irritated my father who had hoped that I would be more courageous in defending myself, destiny had graciously rewarded me for this humility by sealing my memories of him with a pleasurable interaction on a morning with a sweet breeze at another white Jordanian courtyard which I will revisit soon. There, my brief conversation with Fadi was an innocent greeting between children in the morning of their lifetime, only to be reminisced now in the stygian night of these memories, in happiness.

The Garden of Gardens St.

The neighborhood surrounding this younger sibling of the Deir al-Latin family was a long street that ostensibly espoused Jordanian modernity not only through the voice of its upper class restaurants, but also computer stores that gave forth floods of entertainment for thousands of Jordanian children, myself included.

This stretch of modernity also dressed itself in a foreign name, Gardens, to further cement its character in the heart of the city of Amman. The road leading to this contemporary flavor of Jordan's capital passes through many concealed pathways and neighborhoods very much akin to the hidden last names of friends and floors of the school in the center of the neighborhood, atop its majestic hill.

But also like my other vague, ambiguous and barely living memories of Jordan, there emerge a few landmarks that graciously persevere to immortalize Gardens street inside me. Ironically, the site which performs this role is a grocery super store named

Safeway. Just as it provided us with sensible provisions, it also nourishes my imagination by hosting the lingering presence of Gardens within it. Not only did the daily travels with my father to Deir al-Latin begin in the modern street with this supermarket, but it remained an incessant crown that greeted my family and countless others during their outings in this side of the city.

I also remember the organs residing inside Safeway; countless families of aisles that presented Jordanians with a glimpse of the West. Like thousands of other Jordanian teenagers, I wandered through Safeway, and its countless cousins throughout Amman, to appraise the most recent video games and entertainment consoles to hit the market. Even if I did not have permission, yet, to purchase these electronic toys, I found joy in the simple act of hoping that I might add them to my collection.

As the six years of our residence in Jordan aged to their final destination, I witnessed the maturation of Safeway, as well, from a young grocery superstore to a sophisticated social experiment that extended its interests to restaurants and the Western delicacy known as donuts. This last artifact emerges now as a vivid memory that was shared between myself and my dear friend 'Adi. Albeit, the exact form and taste of those donuts disappears now in exchange for the mounting stature of the superstore in a dark Jordanian night enlivened by street lights and family outings.

Other than this biography of a superstore, the genealogical parade of roads and directions leading from our home atop the mountain of Husayn to Safeway vanishes now like the other catacombs within Hashemite monasteries and last names of friends tethered to my memories of Jordan. Nevertheless, the sudden and vivid serenade of images beginning with the contours of this superstore signal the beginning of a long caravan of immortal traces of Gardens and all that it contains of restaurants that have graciously hosted my body and, in return, continue to live as an eternal guest in my past.

There are a few landmarks in this street that appear and request their memory to be commemorated in this journal. Perhaps, their appeal is an attempt to survive the demise of their architectural bodies with which has also died the countless nightly conversations that accompanied feasting on traditional Jordanian delicacies. Or, perhaps, their appeals are an emphasis of their continuous life ... as they demand that I repay their priceless debts, like elders who remind you through their haunting fragility of the transmission of power, strength and spirit which they granted to you epochs ago. In this way, as you live through them, they also demand to live through you.

The most august architectural contours that emerge now from the remnants of this street's memories are that of al-Mu'tasim, a large bakery and desert shop in the heart of Gardens. The presence of this restaurant in my memory serendipitously coincides with its name, al-Mu'tasim, or one who seeks refuge; for that perfectly describes its performance as it melds its' virginal self behind the veils of memories, to become an indispensable, yet subtle, manifestation of my identity.

I know with conviction that this bakery was our regular destination when we, as a family, desired to have a family outing. However, I barely remember a single such occurrence and its exact vicissitudes, much like those lost friends from Tlaa' al-'Ali whose faces haunt me now like apparitions without names.

I do remember one such visit, which is immortalized by an unusual catalyst: the presence of an exchange student from the Caucuses, who was also attending Deir al-Latin. Although his initial bodily appearance at the time seemed haphazard, now his estranged identity eloquently symbolizes the metaphysics of my own migrant soul. Like my compatriot from the Caucuses, the only constancy emerging from this journal is the instability of migration and movement. Seeking the hope of a final destination of tranquility amidst silence, while also having the conviction of being sought after by a relentless past.

As this student sat with his family, in what seemed to be the only few moments of tranquility and certainty amidst countless other blinks of ravaging cultural shocks and unkind shenanigans of teenagers towards another peer of their age from a foreign land, I perceive his vivid face now in complete silence, like those many other friends who are also drowned in the calmness of ambiguity and time. What is important is his inevitable presence, and nobody else's, in the expansive veranda of al-Mu'tasim. I seek refuge, like him, in his tranquility within the embraces of this aging bakery and gladly continue to host him and his family in my heart and mind.

In close proximity to al-Muʿtasim resided Jabri, an old bastion of Jordanian hospitality. Unlike it's culinary sibling, this restaurant engulfed the entirety of Amman in countless branches and endless assortment of dishes that recounted the entire history of Jordanian food in the unsurprising immediacy of Arabian hospitality. This is perhaps why news has reached me recently that al-Mu'tasim's body has disintegrated into the abyss of memories while Jabri remains a standing ovation to this Middle Eastern country's history and heritage, for through its comprehensive offerings of Jordanian foods, it also alludes to its more subtle appreciation of the sweet and somber experiences needed for one to identify with a society.

However, like al-Mu'tasim, my memories here also linger at the shore of ambivalence and ambiguity. The certainty of Jabri's immense role as a bastion of Jordanian hospitality in my childhood is creatively married to the contravening absence of numerous incidents whence it hosted me, save one such instance that has also become immortalized through a peculiar catalyst: the presence of another Iraqi migrant family whom we have invited to this restaurant.

The importance of food and its ability to linger in memory as a transcendent and transient trace of the past cannot be overestimated. My infatuation, as a child, with the *freika bil-dajaj*, Chicken with cracked wheat, which was a staple dish at Jabri, lingered in memory well after my transitory migration in America, whence I tried my best to reproduce this dish in my new home. Unfortunately, such a project has been to no avail, for it is not the content of the ingredients that is missing, but the childhood which initially fostered it

173

that is now separated by an indomitable abyss known as time.

And so, as an adult, I recognize that this is ultimately a coercive projection of a certain enchantment upon my childhood, one that is inevitably gone. Nevertheless, I still choose to undergo the necessary impossible craze of an artist attempting to produce something from nothing. From such boundless separations between oneself and the homeland emerge the oceans of possible negotiations needed for a migrant to traverse the impossible and return to their vanished home from the comfort of their own toiled selves.

A third, albeit more humble, restaurant now also recounts its debts upon my childhood in Jordan. Abbood is a staple *ful we falafel*, fava beans and falafel folk restaurant in Gardens. For one reason or another, I see it now engaging in countless conversations with Deir al-Latin Tlaa' al-Ali, across from the school, on the foot of its hill. And yet, my mind also convinces me that Abbood resided in an altogether different street that branched off the central artery of Gardens.

Altogether, I'm certain that the falafel sandwich stall, which ornamented the Hashemite branch of Deir al-Latin is the cause of this creative migration of Abbood from its original location next to this same school's younger sibling in Tlaa' al-Ali.

Much like al-Mu'tasim and Jabri, I'm also impoverished here of specific instances of eating at this restaurant, save also one visit which took place at night, during which the entire city comes to life in conversations specifically destined for distant memories. From among the countless dishes which Abbood served, one single anomaly remains as its most delicious apparition: an oversized crispy falafel stuffed with spicy red onions. Unfortunately, like Jabri's *frieka bil-Dajaj*, Abbood's oversized spicy falafels also remain an impossible project from the past.

Our last stop in Gardens is not a restaurant, but a store that satiated the needs of every child in Amman at the time: the computer and video game store al-Ghazal. While al-Aqsa store satisfied my needs for console video games, like Super Nintendo and PlayStation, al-

Ghazal was my destination for computer entertainment, a machine which we owned, for the first time, in 1994.

That lavish, white-marbled, computer store next to our apartment in the neighborhood of Husayn supplied us with that first computer. Although primitive according to every standard of technology today, it bore many more fruits of enjoyment and sweet solitude than many of the powerful pieces of hardware and software today that contend with reality itself in their virtual prowess of graphics and processing speed.

And yet, it is worthwhile lingering for brief moments and wonder why did those early days that brandished tediously slow internet speeds, which we did not even have for many years after buying our first computer, low graphic quality or processing clocks still granted us – or me at least – more enjoyment than this current age of fast and fastidious technical pleasures? In many ways, the answer to this dilemma is no different than the paradox of nostalgia and separation governing the symphony of this diary.

I remember, vividly, watching at al-Aqsa store the introductory cinematic to Resident Evil, a PlayStation game which launched in 1996 and was considered at the time the first horror-survival video game of its kind. The immersive experience of witnessing actual film actors in a video game simply cannot be repeated. On the one hand, it seemed to bridge a cultural gap which children my age had regarded, until that point, to be indomitable. On the other hand, it expanded the frontiers of our imagination to what is still possible in the beyond.

However, the 'resident' reality remained that, whatever this possibility for improvement in the quality of video games or technology generally at the time, was still separated from us and distant, in the unknown. As a child, however, I was simply not concerned with such inevitability, only the inimitability of the moment and very visceral experience of being immersed in it completely. In this way, my amour for video games and technology during those childhood years in Jordan, and my current retrospective enchantment and poetic aggrandizement of that aspect of the past is itself exemplary of this entire journal's attempt to assess the anguish of my movement across the oceans of time, space and emotions.

And so, al-Ghazal store emerges in the center of Gardens as a meeting place where all my memories of computer games convalesce comfortably in an aroma of old age. Like Resident Evil, this electronics store serenaded my life with numerous staples of 90's entertainment, such as Tomb Raider and Broken Sword. Each of these video games transforms now into a vortex of merry meetings with friends … each virtual plot converses with a synopsis from my childhood to render this affair of memory and imagination tangible and visible.

One friend who shared with me the hospitality of al-Ghazal is another companion whose first name, Tamer, is orphaned of a last name. As a Christian, he represents the subsisting Christic spirits accompanying my childhood as an Arab Muslim migrant. However, Tamer also conjures other events and places of my childhood in Amman that remain to be discussed in later chapters.

For now, we reminisce about a singular moment when I took Tamer and his father to al-Ghazal to look for computer games. The small meandering contours of the store filled with copies of original games, which the store sold for a fraction of the original price, contrasts with the ancient, vast and yellow-hued home of this Christian family. Transitioning from their traditional home to this store dispensing modern technology in one of the most luxurious streets of Amman at the time felt like a time travel episode from Late Antiquity to a world riddled with Enlightenment. This was masterfully performed, I realize now, by the elderly face of Tamer's father and young female face of the store's owner, both of whom argued during their first encounter due to the Christian parent's perception that the young entrepreneur was disrespectful in her neglect of customers.

The absolved look on her face reveals much more about the state of Gardens that hosted this incident in my heart and mind. I heard some years ago that the Jordanian government had outlawed the sale of any and all copied games and media. This does not actually threaten the fate of al-Ghazal, for the store and its ambiance is safe in my imagination. Rather, it eloquently highlights the spiritual declarations of my own inner government: it has also declared all forged forms and images banished from the kingdom of consciousness, what remains are enchanted remains of a past in transition and clues of unfinished friendships.

The Last Apartment in Gardens St.

Like the sojourn of birth in Baghdad, my childhood in Jordan also found its way to a final residence. Unlike the two previous abodes atop hospitable mountains of Amman, this recently built apartment in Gardens street had to compromise its advantage of contemporary design and new age for a dearth of memories as it barely housed our bodies that had already been destined to leave Jordan for the New World in a short while.

The sudden moments and days leading to our transition from our apartment in the neighborhood of atop the mountain of Husayn to this new, and final, apartment, is as ambiguous now as the unexpected and rapid developments I became accustomed to, already during our final days in Husayn, that our immigration application to America had been accepted and our traversal of the great seas of the world was, momentarily, inevitable.

Like Tamer and his family whose apparitions share our reflections on the nostalgia for Jordanian technology, an Iraqi family hosts serenades and ushers my family's transition into this last apartment in Jordan. Like my parents, this family also flew with the wings of despair from their residence in Iraq to Jordan, and later to Canada.

Our relationship with this company is a vivid landmark of our entire residence in Jordan. Much like us, they transitioned through various stations that also resembled the age and spirit of each of these three residences. Their first home, a sibling of ours atop the mountain of Tariq, speaks to me now of the memories of its blue and red hues and tightly compartmentalized wings that emphasize an architectural kinship.

Their second abode, an ancient space hidden within a maze of greenery bounded by a large courtyard, is an ostensible homage to our aging apartment atop the mountain of Husayn. Much like the staircase descending into the sanctuary of the Hashemite monastery of Deir al-Latin, here also one finds a wrinkled stone staircase descending into this family's residence. Meanwhile, both the Hashemite monastery and this home share the ornament of greenery which greets the visitor of our apartment building atop the mountain of Husayn in the form of a delicate arbor.

And so, it is during our sojourn in this second, aging, residence that both our families agreed to move to two neighboring apartments in a brand new complex on Gardens street. As the Jordanian family whose son that happens to be an architect ventured a new urban life through this investment, our share in these newly born buildings was an elusive beginning for a another migration on the horizon.

Much like the Baghdadian breezes that ornamented our white palatial apartment on Haifa St., this Jordanian sibling also foretold of an imminent departure, one that paradoxically, yet unsurprisingly, breathed its presence through the clothing of modernity and luxury. For it merely performed the lavish yet fleeting siren songs at the summit of this world's pleasures.

The days prior to our actual migration from the mountain of Husayn to Gardens St. witnessed many friendly conversations and plans with our future neighbors as well as witnessing the molding of our, then, unfinished and not yet born new residence. The hammer blows and dust filling the ether of our luxurious kitchen painted in my mind an image of a universe still coalescing through the divine breaths of glorious manifestations, each of which must have also appeared as dancing specks of primordial dust in a vast expanse of nothingness.

The moving day across the terrain of the elder mountain of Husayn to the younger neighborhood of Gardens was one during which much of our furniture tasted the agony and pain of short-term migration. I remember one specific incident, during which a large wooden cabinet was almost broken in half by the worker of the moving company. And yet, like the fast-moving waves of diaspora, they could not care less for another family's belongings, much like those metaphysical breezes of exodus also overwhelm the young and old alike in their swift orders of eviction from normalcy and comfort.

In many ways, even the physical contours of this last apartment reminisce of our white palace on Haifa street. The main doors open to an immediate hallway that speaks of familial privacy. Immediately to the right, there resided the guest room, completely secluded from the rest of the house and its mundane affairs. Expectedly, the windows overlooking the street in this public quarter reveals itself now as larger in size than its previous life, bringing to the forefront its role as the isthmus between the guest room and the endless Jordanian breezes of hospitality.

The spatial rank of this room, in relation to the rest of the house, is itself a narrative that began with the guest room on Haifa street, matured atop the mountain of Husayn and reached old age in the young neighborhood adjacent to Gardens street. In its youth, in Baghdad, our guest room opened its arms wide to the family room and spacious balcony overlooking the famous street filled with European architecture.

As it matured and experienced the estrangement of migration and departure, the guest room chose a smaller and more secluded location in our first and second abode in Amman that solely embraced the living room. This increasing longing for privacy emerged perhaps as a result of the preceding diaspora, an estrangement that appeared, architecturally, as a spatial symbol of the hidden desires of the recluse, simultaneously filtering foreignness to seek instead intimacy with the familial and familiar.

And so, by the time this quarter of hospitality reaches the newly born apartment in Gardens, it manifests its elderly experience through a total seclusion from the rest of the house. The conversations and whispers of visitors did not mingle with the nightly conversations of close family and friends. Not only was this seclusion a natural development of the 'growing pains' of an unfinished Iraqi childhood in Jordan, but also a foreshadowing of the imminent departure towards the West; a new form of journey whose spirit had been imprinted through vast traversals of terrain through the years.

This is the story of an immediate right turn at the hallway greeting the front door of our new apartment. Turning left, we are met with a humble family room and kitchen that embraced one another in testimony to the merger of Iraqi, Egyptian and Jordanian hospitalities. And yet, as is the case with most of the places I have described thus far, there are no distinct breaths that give these corners any human life. Instead, also like the other spaces I have mentioned, it is the very ether of structures, their textures and colors that grant them a special imaginal life.

Undoubtedly, this scarcity of human traces in this last apartment is augmented by the brief blinking moments we spent there. The main memories waving their aura as I write this memoir now are the faces of our Iraqi neighbors who transitioned with us into this complex and who visited us often. It was an Iraqi companionship on the verge of continuing its travels away from this Jordanian transit.

The seclusion that sanctified the virginity of the guest room, and also guarded the familial aura of the kitchen and living room, likewise granted the bedrooms their own distinct ambiance that differed from the rest of the house. From this imaginal perspective, this portion of this last apartment in Gardens St. pays homage to its ancestor in Haifa street. And yet, my memory leaves no traces now of this part of the house save a few glimpses of my bedroom. All other forms, events and moments that had taken place in those hallways have already migrated towards an unknown future.

Isn't it remarkable that the longest living memories of this home is the most public and secluded of quarters, the guest room? Then, like separation from the source of fragrance, the traces vanish slowly towards the most private of rooms, culminating in an almost unrecognizable apparition of the bedrooms, bereft of any human imprints. However, this should not be surprising, since migration slowly and painfully skins privacy out of its subjects, either through the disparagement of their identities and memories, rendering them no different than their luggage and clutters, or through their own necessary sacrifice, when they slaughter these belongings and consciousness away from privacy into public life, in order to forge a narrative of the anguish of diaspora and exile.

As I try to think of any other possible memories that emanate from the vicinities of this house, my heart orders me to direct my attention instead to the local mosque in the neighborhood. Although the happenings at such a place deserve an entire chapter, as has been our tradition in previous parts of this book, the dearth of memories in this last apartment and immortal influence which this mosque has had on my life harmonize into a singular abode that extends from the walls of a newly born apartment into the vicinity embracing Gardens street.

I mostly attended this mosque, which resided at the end of the street to our house, on Fridays for the special sermon. My attendance of these religious services during this period of my life was mostly ceremonial and compulsory. As will become clearer in later chapters, my genuine exploration of the spiritual chasm of myself occurred later on, in America and sustained by separation from all things Islamic.

And yet, I found the first glimpses of what would become my spiritual identity during these weekly visits to the local mosque nearby our last Jordanian apartment. During the earliest such visit that I can remember, the *mu'adhdhin*, or person who made the call to prayer, proceeded to melodiously serenade every corner of the mosque and our neighborhood with his *adhan*, call to prayer.

When he reached the second iterations of the verse, *hayya ala-l-salat*, "come to prayer", and *hayya ala-l-falah*, "come to prosperity", my tears suddenly came to life and immediately migrated down to the dark green carpet covering the floor of the prayer hall, thereby marrying the body of the mosque and immortalizing this incident. It was in itself a transcendent experience since I realized that my ingestion of the sacred nature of this liturgy surpassed the boundaries of my mind and lingered in the center of my heart whence it became a direct conversation between the melody which clothed the verses and the meaning generated by this music.

The power of this experience is augmented by the fact that my comprehension and awareness of the musicality of the man's recitation was still an illiterate, primordial and quite raw delicacy. When such experiences overwhelm you, they do not distinguish between any of your senses. They actually overwhelm all these windows into your soul along with every atom in your being all at once, at the price of rendering you unable to control or subject this deluge of feelings to the governance of your mind and reason.

With this first encounter, the ground was settled and paved for my lifelong journey with my faith Islam, in musical, as opposed to legalistic or theological steps. The first tear I shed for God, emanated because He spoke to me in a somber melody through the veil of an unknown *mu'adhdhin* in one of the countless, and similarly humble, mosques of Amman.

And yet, I had no awareness of the reason or definition of this melody which so chained me within its rapturous ocean. This would become another efflorescence that I would grow with in America, to be

191

discussed at a later time and place. But it is here, in this local mosque in Jordan that my first actual meeting with God took place, through this somber siren song of the heavens.

And it is also this sentiment which I, at the time, understood to the extent that it evoked within me tremendous anguish. Later on, when I discovered the realm of *maqamat*, or different modalities in Arabic music, I also understood the divine purpose behind my exposure to this character of a melody during that period of my childhood, exemplified by my tearful reaction: it was a watershed moment of my growth into a life of nostalgia, separation and diaspora.

In deeper terms, the tears that flowed from within were themselves the symbolic respiration of my spirit as it came to terms, through its marriage with this melody, of the single constancy that it will have during the coming years and lifetime: a traversal across regions, seas and lands that further segment my identity across the spectrum of a past more faded and missed in its own childhood.

It is also not surprising that this encounter with the language of heavens, music, occurred in the vicinity of our last apartment in Jordan, just prior to an irreversible migration to an altogether different hemisphere. If my departure from Iraq was towards a close neighbor, then my looming travel was an entire exodus from an Arab embrace towards a Western myth of glory ... or so I thought at the time.

Education in the Inner Sanctum of al-'Abdali

Like our previous two homes in Amman, our last apartment in Gardens was married to a new monastery of education. Through one mirror, I had migrated away from the family of Deir al-Latin, which had hosted me previously in the Hashemite district and Tlaa' al-'Ali. Through another, grander mirror, I had remained under the auspices of Christian care and tutelage.

Towards the end of our school year in Tlaa' al-'Ali, many of my peers had begun to hope to attend one of the luxurious high schools in Amman. My fate, through my own choice, resided upon the name of a school which I had regularly heard from many of the students as being the most prestigious of these secondary educational institutions, Terra Sancta college.

Prior to being admitted to this school, those of us who wished to be admitted had to have an entry examination. Much of the proceedings of this ritual escape me now. However, one detail remains pertaining to an English reading examination which I had in a small office at the end of an otherwise vast hallway. In reality, as will become clear momentarily, Terra Sancta's main classroom building was a massive hall of hallways, a maze of classrooms and it continues to expand in glory due to the machinations of nostalgia and imagination.

Perhaps, the reason why I remember this small detail is the actual result of the reading examination which allowed me to be admitted into the college, due to my exceptional reading skills in English. A pleasant surprise which, also perhaps, was a divine foreshadowing of the aid that English will provide me in the future as a medium of expressing a longing that cannot be contained within words, for a past that transcends the life of ink and paper.

Like a dream, I cannot remember the first day of attending Terra Sancta, nor the last moments for that matter. The first disappearance is unexplainable, while the latter is probably instigated by our initial visit to

America during the Christmas vacation of 1996. In between these two abysses of absence, every corner of Terra Sancta conjures up endless moments of a high school life that continuously demand recollection and memorialization.

Like the school days of Deir al-Latin, in both the Hashemite district and Tlaa' al-'Ali, the ride to and from school is part of its ambiance in the imagination of a child. Just as the vast roads connecting the mountain of Tariq to the Hashemite district are creative extensions of an aging monastery and the luxurious restaurants of Gardens ornament the foothold of the hill upon which stands the monastery of Tlaa' al-'Ali, likewise, here also the inroads from the hustle and bustle of al-'Abdali also take one on a steep climb up the mountain of Leweibdah, where Terra Sancta stands as the crown at the peak.

And yet, unlike the clear visions I continue to have of the roads connecting the mountain of Tariq to the Hashemite district, my memory of the streets connecting Gardens to al-'Abdali is as treacherous as my recollection of the beginning of the former road of luxury: a remembrance that dies at the sight of a massive shopping complex called Safeway.

The meandering path up this mountain was made less daunting by the numerous ornamentations of houses, mosques and churches that rendered the mountain as friendly as a hill, no different than the mountains of Tariq and Husayn that have hid their elevation within a humility of hospitality and tradition. This domesticating effect of the ornamentation on the mountain also created a pleasurable anticipation as one found their way to the crown of education atop the peak. Like a proper maze, the school had various entrances as well. Each of these gateways revealed an aspect of Terra Sancta's indomitable expanse.

Ironically, the main entrance was one that we the students rarely entered. Rather, like the main door to a home followed by a guest room, this entrance was also reserved for visitors. On the other hand, the side entrance, through which the school buses carrying us embraced the inner sanctum and courtyard, was akin to a special entrance to a home, reserved for family and friends. Of course, these multiple entrances were also a unique gift granted to Terra Sancta above the previous siblings of Deir al-Latin, highlighting not only this college's larger spatial imprint, but also the growth of life that it ushers into the lives of the students who transition into its care from the previous stage of childhood.

The school buses which carried us from our homes to this inner sanctum of the school were, as I mentioned, an indivisible experience from the school itself. They were moving extensions of the architectural space … or at least that is how they appear to me now in my imagination. Added to this mobility is the unique emblem which Terra Sancta had obtained as the school which overlapped my residence in two apartments, atop the mountain of Husayn and Gardens. As the journey in the early morning from each house to the school differed drastically from the other, it also further emphasized the seemingly endless expanse of the school.

It occurs to me now that each of these journeys begin in a manner that also mirrors its reality as an extension of the school itself. The first began at the end of the green-lit road leading to our apartment in the mountain of Husayn. Every morning, the bus stopped across from the rush of taxis that congregated, illegally, only to be fined by police officers a few moments later. This was but a miniature reenactment of the entire Abdali valley upon which rested the mountain of Leweibdah that housed Terra Sancta. However, the small and illegal nature of the taxi stop across our house is met here with a the larger and more official stature of taxi gathering in al-'Abdali.

As for the second journey, from our last apartment in Gardens, it performs instead the mountainous trek up the slope of Leweibdah in its similar terrain from our house, which also rested atop one of the hills surrounding Gardens. Like the meandering trek from al-'Abdali to Terra Sancta, the hill which housed our last apartment also entertained many traversals from the fortress of the housing complex to the outside and brimming life of the city. Although, many of these paths, like other contours of Gardens, also elude my memory now. From this perspective, the hill and neighborhood which this last apartment has occupied in my imagination is similar to our first home atop the mountain of Tariq, also fortified by an abyssal valley decorated with orchards. Here, however, this gorge is one of forgetfulness and longing.

Returning to the crown atop the mountain of Leweibdah, the daily bus ride from our homes to the inner sanctum of Terra Sancta are culminated by a banner that spells the name of the school in an archway that reminisced of the lost traces of great civilizations in the palaces of Granada and Cordova. Especially now, in the court of memory and imagination, not only does the form of these ancient castles union with the archway of Terra Sancta, but also the smell and texture of the ether collapse the separation in epochs of a creative performance.

The tight embrace of the archway, which barely allows for the buses to pass through opens to what seems like an endless courtyard, boundaryless like the ambitions of school children. In some ways, this vast courtyard was an entire neighborhood that encompasses what resided outside the walls of the other schools I attended in Amman. Also, in contrast to the falafel stall that stood outside the Hashemite monastery, the restaurant in Terra Sancta was located alongside this wall guarding the school's large courtyard. It faced inwardly towards the boundaryless sanctum.

Alongside the courtyard stood a short fence, contending with the seemingly endless walls that surrounded the sacred valley in the Hashemite monastery. Its humble stature was by no means a show of weakness. Rather, it allowed through and embraced the ancient Jordanian breezes, transcending the age of Arabs and Islam to Byzantium and the foregone eras. It permitted these faded entries with an aura of confidence that foretold its understanding of their origins and had the expansive heart to embrace their present realities.

The ability of Terra Sancta to undertake this timeless project was proven daily through the countless number of students that walked through this vast courtyard. Alongside this flow of bodies resided endless other oceans of conversations, beneath which lingered folds within folds of pearls made of dreams, ambitions and streams of thoughts. Some of which surfaced through the blind determination of children while others sadly sacrificed themselves at the blunt altar of adulthood.

Others still tried to remain hidden within the hearts and consciousness of these school children, hoping for a moment when their mature sensibilities succumbs, once again, to their child-like spontaneity. It waits patiently for the moment when that pure, innocent and illiterate ambition is dressed in a bodily garb of a matured body with uncanny acumen.

I say this now as I remember my own conversations with friends who treaded the monasterial paths across the vast terrain of this courtyard. Here appears a conversation about a watch which an eccentric friend asked to borrow and refused my refusal. Elsewhere, in the corner by a nameless wall, emerges another chatter about video games that were still newborn at the time but which are now aging and decrypt in the 21st century. Ultimately, these last few paragraphs which I have just written are precisely the objective of this journal: to render the mundane breaths and trivial concerns of school children a testimony for the sanctity of time itself in the court of human imagination.

In the center of this vast courtyard began the architectural transition to the heart of the school, wherein resided the classrooms and hallways of endless memories. As for the architectural transition, this appeared in an enclosure with pillars that shielded students from the sun and compensated them for the seemingly eternal moments we had to stand during the morning salute for the national anthem. In many ways, this enclosure embodied through its architectural liminality, between indoors and outdoors, the endless puzzles of migration. For brief moments, every morning, all the students in Terra Sancta stood solemnly to pay tribute to the Jordanian national anthem; all the while, they also experienced a certain stillness of also lingering at faded boundaries between countries and their identities ... between nationalisms and imagined nationalities.

Towards the far end of the courtyard, at the other side of the seminal horizon from the archway that welcomed the school buses, there resided a secluded gym that I rarely frequented. My detest for team sports was doubtlessly influenced by my awareness and attraction to the loneliness embedded in diaspora and its impeccable mirroring of the human journey. Nevertheless, there was once held a science fair in this gym at which I prepared and presented a crystal prism that split a light source into countless rays of colors. The story of my project and participation in this fair is unusually peculiar and pertinent to the overall itinerary of this journey, and so I will mention it here.

It is indeed rare that people, including myself, should play an important role in this journal where buildings and spaces have been the central protagonists, they are the ones who speak through their textures, colors and faded aspects. Even in this particular case, the conversations, interactions and arguments all flow to the valley of this lonely gym's texture and old age. It is in such an ancient dress right now, within the confines of my memory, that it consumes all the events that occurred between its walls and renders them completely still and silent, no different than any of the other wrinkles on its concrete-like skin.

I had prepared my large cardboard with a small crystal prism situated at the top left corner, glued securely to its place. A small flashlight was stationed just above the prism, right at the corner of the cardboard. Together, the crystal prism and light source unleashed a companionship of colored rays that dwarfed, in their breadth and depth, the small physical stature of the prism. I realize now also that, like all things in my story, this simple science project bears endless streams of metaphors. In other words, a prism on a cardboard from the 90's is itself a timeless prism residing on the endless expanse of imagination and channeling endless rays of meanings through the light of creative inspiration.

Unfortunately, my project was lost, at the behest of bad management and handling. My science teacher, who had coordinated and sponsored my project was thoroughly upset and blamed absent-mindedness on all sides. The same reaction could be perceived in my father who, for a little while, swore he would never help me prepare this project again. When he had realized that such an approach would prove fruitless in bringing justice to this lost prism and its colored feathers of light, he decided to build another one. This time, it was imprinted with the intention that it be destined to fall into the hands of a trusted science teacher.

As the proverb says, "When I do something good, no one remembers. When I do something bad no one forgets". My memory is no exception in this case, since no recollection remains of the surviving iteration of this science project. The only faded images that subsist are of me standing in the secluded and aging gym explaining how a prism works to passersby. And so, spreading forth the images and events surrounding the first broken prism and its surviving sibling, the older brother receives a recompense for its short life in a more condensed and fleshed out tragedy, whereas the younger one is humbled by a more faded and short life in the land of memories.

Returning the interstice between the courtyard and hallways of learning in Terra Sancta, there are numerous memories that linger in just this part of the school. Ironically, very few of them involve the daily tribute to the Jordanian anthem and flag, for which this expanse was entirely designed. Rather, I see now a trickster peer of my graduating class, whose physical compromise was his rather short stature, having a good time kicking taller students, such as myself, in order to feel a brief sense of triumph. His gloat manifested in a giggle he uttered loudly with every tall student that he managed to bring to their knees.

I also see myself conversing with my English teacher, who found pride in the fact that she taught and spoke British English, as opposed to its 'broken American mutation' across the ocean. I specifically remember recounting to her some British jokes I had read in a book once, hoping to see her laugh. Instead, all I received was a smile. However, this hardly meant, for me at the time, that she did not enjoy the joke or did not have a sense of humor. Rather, it was the same smile she granted when one of her students succeeded or did something well. This was her way of letting me know that she is happy because my initial trip to America had not ruined my tutelage in English that I received at her hands.

This teacher, whose name now escapes me like many other teachers and friends before, had a sister who was a teacher of geography and social science at Terra Sancta. Together, they covered nearly the entire spectrum of topics that students needed to learn at that age. Their faces appear to me so clearly now. The English teacher eloquently performed the stereotypical image, which Arabs have in their mind of a Western lady, with her blond hair. Her sister, on the other hand, wore the blackest of hair colors; a contrast which nicely reflects the difference in their teaching focus. It is not so much that black hair signified Jordan, but when compared to the blondness of the English teacher, their emerges in this sibling's black hair a symbolism of tradition and heritage, if only in this context.

This metaphorical mirroring is augmented by the fact that, during my studies at Terra Sancta in the 90's, these teachers were already in their 60's or 70's. I am constantly humbled and made somber by the fact that not only have they retired from teaching at the school, but most likely their bodies have also retired from carrying and imprisoning their spirits in this world and have, thus, returned to the great beyond. It is in the face of this sobering reality that I try to hold on to every wrinkle and smile on their faces, word of encouragement or discipline they hurled at me … even the way they addressed other students I consider now an art work that has surpassed in its age the requirement for a copyright or trademark. It has become a memory free of any royalty, brandished by the blemishes from my own imagination.

And yet, something else reappears to me here and now which I have not had the chance to discuss beforehand. It is truly wonderous, this affair of imagination and memory, how it renders the minute details of events, persons and places from the past so much more vivid, even in the face of the most ruthless waves of amnesia and forgetfulness. As aware as I feel in this instance of the intricate manner in which these two sibling teachers spoke and walked, I'm not sure I was as certain of this during my time at Terra Sancta.

The few people I seem to remember in the course of writing this autobiography seem to re-emerge in a similar manner to the countless buildings and spaces that I remember even better. The question that keeps arising every time I contemplate this side of the ocean of memory and imagination is, are these extra details a tributary of my childhood and the pure experience of life at the time or my current adulthood and my increasingly cerebral and heart-wise awareness of that past? Will the same costume of vivid details also be dressed upon the memories of persons and events from my life now, when I attempt to wipe away the dust of time to converse with them again, some thirty years later?

Marching forth towards the classrooms is a ceremonial process from the transitory part of the courtyard towards the inner enclave. The ceremony was somewhat short-lived and involved a staircase that descended from the front door of the main building towards the courtyard on the either side, like wings of a figurative bird carrying the ascending and descending students on its back. Immediately facing this ornamented gate is the other, main, entrance to the school which, as we have already mentioned, was rarely used by the family members of the school, its students and faculty.

Like an auspicious and spacious home, the guest room of Terra Sancta connected to its living quarters, the inner sanctum courtyard, through a humble lobby which contained the offices of the principal and secretary. Retreating our steps back towards the living room entrance, my memory concedes now that there was something to be found on the immediate right of the hallway that meets us when we enter through these doors. Unfortunately, this same memory deceives me also with a faded image ornamented by blinding light that gently turns me away from a part of Terra Sancta that has been locked away from me within the confines of my own conscience.

Immediately to the left, however, is where our journey continues in this tight hallway further restricted by its disappearing architecture in my memory. Our daily journeys towards the classrooms, which resided in the upper floors of the main building, proceeded through the main staircase in this side of the hallway. Like an entire film reel collapsed into a single frame, I see myself now walking among the endless procession of students in the morning and after the mid-noon lunch break. I also see this march occurring in all four seasons at once. The dark grey and aging steps of the staircase reveal their clear crevices in the dry heat of summer and the wintery puddles of water that smoothly veil that old age like a magical skin cream. Somewhat haphazardly, this entire ruckus of the four seasons only emerges now so that I can remember cowboy-like brown boots which I used to wear during the winter treks up the staircase of this crown atop the summit of Leweibdah.

I seem pretty certain, notwithstanding the connivance of separation and memory, that there was only a second floor to the main building. Exiting the staircase delivers you to a spacious hallway. At one end of this hallway, to the left, resides the small office which still attests to my ability in reading English. Many of the rooms that hosted the years I spent at Terra Sancta lingered around this office. This is hardly surprising; for like a hospitable patron, this office strived to keep me in close proximity to its premises.

Here emerges also another mirroring difference between East and West ... between Terra Sancta and its counterparts in America. During my childhood in Iraq and Jordan, it was customary for students to remain in the same classroom for the duration of the school year, and to be visited by different teachers throughout the day. In America, prior to beginning my first school year, there was an overwhelming anxiety anticipating my necessary transition from one room to the next. The teachers in the New World remain in stasis and students seek them in constant movement. In the East, on the other hand, the roles were reversed, and it was the students who remained still while teachers sought them.

Fortunately, memory and the past suspend judgment in the presence of art ... they do not attempt to place these two pairs of movement and stillness in contention with one another, only completion and harmony. Like yin and yang, students and teachers in Jordan and America come together for a grand narrative in my conscience. I am not so much opting for a denial of differences as I am sacrificing them at the altar of perplexity, so that they reveal their true purpose in a greater perspective. If Terra Sancta, its teachers and courtyards, can coexist alongside my high school and college education in America, then surely such a grand narrative was deemed possible by the divine hand of destiny.

The classrooms in Terra Sancta were spacious, probably more so now in my imagination than their original physical condition. The walls, like those in the other schools I attended, spoke of their old age and experience. The light brown hue of these embracing arms of the rooms melds now with a marble flooring that danced between infinite shades of browns and greys. The distance between the blackboard and desks of the students also expands now in this journey to the past. It stretches until it renders the entire room an ancient theater where immortal actors addressed their attentive audience from a stage that seemed to stretch for horizons with no end.

I'm assuming now, due to the deception of memory and its lack of trustworthiness, that the vivid Jordanian sun filled both the ethers of time and space in these rooms, like an experienced director who orchestrated the tragedies and comedies of life and death in those ancient theaters. Perhaps that sun, that still shines now across the seas, in Jordan, and America where I reside, foretold my need to remember those foregone days under her auspices in Terra Sancta.

This is hardly a difficult feat of hospitality, however, for an entity that has witnessed lifetimes of childhoods. Indeed, for the sun, the ocean of letters that brings this journal to life is but a speck of movement in its lifetime.

As a constant monument to unfathomable energy and movement, it is also a testimony to longevity that emanates and lingers around impeccable stillness. Like an experienced elder, who witnesses the foolishness of those who have not tasted life yet with a gentle smile and serene body, the sun resides solemnly facing the thrones of life and death, and attests to crashing waves of both bodies and memories at the shores of these twin theaters.

And so, the sun knows, better than me, the narratives of breaths at Terra Sancta before and after me. It is indeed wondrous, that one who is distant from me beyond countability knows the governing motions of my childhood in Jordan and is able to witness that symphony in much better clarity than I ever will. That is also a part of art, its gentle crushing force that humbles you into acquiescing your inability to conquer your desires and sustains your power to long for and seek that impossible destination. The most sobering aspect of this realization is that the sun actually remembers the names that accompany the faces of my old friends who have escaped my feeble but longing heart.

I would like to turn to those faces that I met at Terra Sancta, some of whom I remember very well while others carry on with the other 'nameless portraits hung in empty halls', as Don McLean tells us of Vincent's memoirs. Other teachers appear to me now, alongside the two sisters who mirrored the east and west. Like the kinship that connected these two women, there was a deeper relationship between my science and math teachers. They were not related by blood, but rather through their specializations that complement each other and eccentric behaviors and voices that have occupied my mind all these years. Even the clothes they wore are now collapsed into a single archetypal set that captures their fashion style and perhaps embodies their personalities.

The only thing I remember from my science teacher's name is Abdullah, 'the servant of God'; a fairly common name in the Arab world. Perhaps it is this abstract adage that allows my teacher's ghost to easily transition into an archetypal role right now in my journey into the past. But it is also the combination of his unique voice, eccentric mannerisms, traditional Palestinian accent and conniving sternness that come together to render him as a memorable character; at least as memorable as the buildings and spaces that occupy the most words and ink in this journal.

He also embodied, in parallel to his performative character, the entire spectrum of the hard sciences. He taught biology for seventh grade, chemistry in eighth grade and whatever else he was capable of conveying to young minds in later years. As I attempt to find any of his pictures on the college's website, I'm immediately reminded, indirectly, of the tremendous effect he had on my last semesters of education in Jordan. The least of these lasting effects is my special affinity to the Palestinian vernacular; a particular way of pronouncing Arabic that renders every Palestinian I meet now a window into that distant past. Incidentally, this is itself a thoroughly artistic state: the way the creative process transforms regular people you meet into oceans of potential artwork.

Professor Abdullah was a celebrity of sorts. His ruthless strictness mixed with his wit and exceptional fashion style to make him an overwhelming presence. We were simultaneously stricken with fear lest we disrespect him or perform weakly in his classes. At the same time, we were involuntarily drawn with our easily impressionable childlike perceptions to his wit and cologne that mixed with chemicals from the science lab. As will become clear during my recount of the transition to America and my continuing education there, I even continued to perceive my Palestinian teacher's apparition in the middle school I attended in the New World. Specifically, his distinct smile seems to have possessed another science teacher in Scarlet Middle school.

A contract remains between this teacher and myself; a chemistry quiz which I failed miserably and anticipated in horror the day he returned the quizzes to the entire class. The overwhelming anxiety was worsened by the fact that he chose to allude to each student's performance, publicly, as he passed back their exam. Then, the statement came, "I'm very sad at how Ali

Hussain performed on this quiz", which humiliated me in front of the students and walls of the classroom that still attest to this incident. However, his remark also revealed his endearing respect; a deference that caused him to express sadness instead of mockery, which largely shaped his commentary of other failed students in the classroom.

Of course, professor Abdullah is also the one who granted my martyred science fair project another sacrifice of ruthless criticism, due to the mishandling of the school staff. In turn, the two iterations of the prism and its rays of light harmoniously embody this teacher's twin mirrors, of a ruthlessness that destroys and impeccable wit that brings to life and assists in survival. Rather, such is the universe and our share of a fleeting life in it. Like the sun that burns all in close proximity to it, a pain expressing its own inner anguish, also serenely sheds its luminosity upon the aging walls of a school like Terra Sancta, so that a migrant school child can remember it for decades of dust and memories.

Alongside the two sisters who mirror East and West and professor Abdullah there is our Math teacher who complemented his counterpart in the hard sciences with an altogether completely different set of eccentricities. The fancy suits of the science teacher contrast with the – now – nameless Math teacher's less formal, but equally savvy, leather jackets and casual shoes. The memorable Palestinian accent of the former teacher also contends with the husky voice and laidback Jordanian vernacular of this Math teacher. Not even their hair was spared this distinction in style. The smoothly combed hair of professor Abdullah, resembling his fancy suits, contrasts with the blunt baldness of the Math teacher, also reflecting its owner's carefree personality.

Unfortunately, like his absent name, I do not have any distinct memories of him. His personality lingers as the only marker of his existence in my life. Perhaps due to a singular incident involving a failed chemistry quiz, a contract with memory, that I remember professor Abdullah more than his teaching-sibling in the Math department. Nevertheless, together, these two teachers embody the brief days I spent at Terra Sancta; stricture coupled with informality, failed experiments followed by their successful descendants. All of this took place as a final sojourn before destiny bid me farewell away from Jordan towards the New World.

And so, my entire educational life in this home away from home took place under the auspices of Christian friars from the Franciscan order. While writing these final statements about Terra Sancta in this chapter, I realized that I had forgetfully omitted any mention of the significance of this religious imprint upon this third monastery in Amman, sitting like a crown atop the mountain of Leweibdah. I then realized that this monasterial spirit is the same aura that runs through the two previous siblings of Deir al-Latin, in the Hashemite district and Tlaa' al-'Ali. Together, Deir al-Latin and Terra Sancta are expressions of a singular meaning of faith that permeates and colors even the memories of a migrant school child who filled his imagination with their ether over two decades ago. Incidentally, this symphony unfolds in the same manner that the disparate places, people and incidents in my memory seem to come together creatively into a divinely choreographed symphony, just as seemingly unrelated words become uttered relatives, through the hospitable kinship of a poem or novel.

The Soft Luxuries of Sweifiyya

I am now attempting to revisit with you as many locations in Amman, sacred to my childhood, as I can before the memory of migration and departure reappears to sweep me away from my second home once again. Destiny works in this way, not even certain memories are stripped of the original anxiety, suddenness and turmoil that surrounded the physical body of the event.

There are only a few places left in Amman that stand in line now between us and the migration that will take us to the conclusion of this book. Sweifiyya is one of these last places that remains in the Amman of my imagination. At the time, during the mid 90's, this neighborhood was one of the wealthiest and most luxurious regions in the outskirts of the Jordanian capital. Long spacious roads with, what now seems to be, white buildings from the boundaries of imagination. I cannot remember exactly which traffic circle inaugurated the beginning of Sweifiyya. However, I do recall that all of Amman is organized

225

around these giant circular islands. The earliest of them, in turn, usher in the oldest neighborhoods in Amman. On the other hand, the one that welcomed visitors into Sweifiyya was of the youngest additions to this family of traffic circles.

And so, in contrast to the mountains of Husayn and Leweibdah or their other siblings, such as the mountain of Amman, where your eyes were met in every direction with tradition in the form of buildings that espoused centuries of experience in their wrinkled texture, Sweifiyya was an open horizon upon which luxury was sprinkled in rarities as an ornament to its spacious roads. Between these glimpses of the rich, there are countless in roads and branches that remind us of the arteries atop the mountain of Tariq; walkways that touch every boundary of the neighborhood, allowing visitors to witness Jordanian hospitality in both its traditional and modern mirrors.

My father used to take us every Friday, the first day of the weekend in the Middle East, to Sweifiyya to have lunch and ice cream. The neighborhood opened its welcoming arms week after week without hesitation. Perhaps because like the other areas of Amman that we lived in and frequented, Sweifiyya also knew that our impending departure is inevitable. Afterall, once you become a migrant, your fate is eternally tied to movement. Your entire being becomes antithetical to the state of stasis. Inwardly and outwardly, you become an embodiment of diaspora. This is not so much the state of not belonging to any place, but the overwhelming anxiety of recognizing that a part of you resides in each of the soils that your body and soul have married. This the anxiety of multiple identities and the riveting creativity born of converging oceans that flow from elsewhere shores. Each of the sandy coasts of these imaginal waters bring breezes that constantly remind of separation.

These are distances that, like the possession of migration, also colonize your body and spirit, space and time, place and memory. The only cause for tranquility while sailing through these unrelenting oceans of creativity are the white pearls at the bottom of the ocean that reveal themselves as constants in a life's journey. In the oceans of my life's incidents, the ceaseless waves give way to the white pearls of spacious courtyards that tie this entire journey together. These same gardens of pure marble reappear now all over Sweifiyya; they carry me back towards the tangible textures of this rich neighborhood of Amman that nourished and witnessed the growth of my childhood every week for many years in the 90's.

Like many of the places in Amman that influence the trajectory of my thoughts until today, the cartography of pathways from our house to Sweifiyya also mystically disappear now from memory. Instead, it appears as a sudden transition traversing vast distances across the city. Our first stop during the regular weekend outings, as well as now in this return journey, is at China Inn, a restaurant that collapsed the abyssal divide between east and west for a few moments every Friday at lunch hour. This should hardly be a surprising conclave for a migrant family. The globalized presence of Chinese food in a luxurious neighborhood of Amman is precisely the type of constancy that people in transition experience all the time. Reference and serenity are found in those signs of the world that also feel out of place. But like the tense oceans of creativity I mentioned above, the silver lining in these stations of diaspora resides in the connections and intimations between the here and there. For migrants, meaning departs from the surface towards the depths above the surface … in these relationships and contexts.

China Inn was a small but cozy restaurant with an ambiance that spoke through reddish hues. My lunch was always the same: noodles with cashew chicken. As much as I anticipated arriving at the restaurant every week in order to enjoy my regular servings of Chinese food, my desire was also to quickly finish my meal and go to the branch of the video game store, al-Aqsa, just around the corner; the same franchise that resided on the other side of Amman, in the more traditional neighborhood of atop the mountain of Husayn. If China Inn closed the gap between east and west into a tight embrace, then al-Aqsa performed the same lullaby, collapsing the separation between Amman's luxurious modernity and traditional heritage into a singular breeze of Jordanian hospitality.

There are so many restaurants and boutiques standing between China Inn and al-Aqsa that I now regret not visiting or paying attention those Fridays, because it was this choice that deprives me now of recounting their names and facial features, like my other half-forgotten friends. The only architectural face I do remember is a spacious restaurant that meets the eye on the way from China Inn to the video game store. I also recall that it was another international sensation that sold Hamburgers, most probably Hardee's.

Amazingly, the texture of the street closer to al-Aqsa seems to my mind's eye now to age quickly, closer to the wrinkles of life's experience that overwhelm the other branch of the video game store atop the mountain of Husayn. This is all the more ironic since this is a store outwardly enmeshed in tradition while inwardly espousing virtual modernity. Like China Inn, and the other al-Aqsa across the city, this branch was also small and cozy, filled to the brim with video games like an ancient library with similar entertaining ink on paper. Between my countless visits to both this branch and its older sibling across the city, I lose track now which games I bought from which brother. Instead, they all harmonize into a single virtual smoke screen of transience; the same impermanence that possesses life itself but is concealed from everyone except those privy to movement and transition.

Continuing down the street from the luxurious sibling of al-Aqsa, you reach with me now a foreign ocean consisting of a wide street filled with restaurants towards the side of our video game store and Chinese restaurant. These restaurants and stores, whose exact number evades me now as it did then, lay under Romanesque pillars that pay homage to the Byzantium that governed the daily affairs of this land long before mosques and minarets. The hazy waves of cars and people serenading that nameless street beckons to my perplexing hesitance to visit that street during my regular Childhood visits. The only restaurant I seem to remember, for no apparent reason, is an ice cream store that lay just around the corner.

And then, beyond this cozy neighborhood of streets and turns, the Sweifiyya of my imagination transitions to another scene, disconnected from the familial restaurant and video game store. What appears to me is the vast promenade of cars surrounded by luxurious palaces on either side of the road ... palaces, I might add, that pay homage to whiteness and purity of wealth. At the end of this seemingly endless highway amidst a neighborhood resided a swimming pool where my brother Muhammad regularly went to swim and coach younger enthusiasts in the art of maneuvering the waves.

I remember one incident when I went with my brother to learn how to swim. I had had a fear of swimming for as long as I can remember; a nice brotherly complement to my elder sibling who was a champion swimmer in Iraq. For him, continuing to teach swimming in Jordan was a way to both earn money and take his inevitable journey of migration to its symbolic end through the waves of water, where no borders or nation-states can be found and no passports are needed to cross from one depth to the other. I watched my brother on that day greet one of his young students who had just finished practicing back and forth in a rote-repetition of fluid movement.

Then, my turn came to jump in the water, and I stood there, still and frozen in fear of the unexpected. My brother grew slowly impatient asking me to dive to unexpected depths, as was my perseverance also dwindling with every moment trying to comprehend my reticence and fear. These types of questions neither require nor need an answer. The fluid motion of meaningful inquiry here resides in the difference between my brother's fearless marriage with water and my respect for this liquid body from afar. If I were to swim back and forth in the pool of this reflection, I find myself at the shore of distinct personalities and different ways of dealing with diaspora.

My brother continued to, and still does, swim towards a meaningful peace his entire life. He realized that movement is the only possible path towards whatever unknown destination resides at the end of the road. He also knew with conviction that leaving one's home is itself an endless ocean of movement: you can only find peace if you move along the signs and vestiges reminding you of distant origins. I, on the other hand, sought refuge through a separated observation, and I still do. I wander outwardly in stillness, and indulge inwardly through rapid ceaseless movement. The thought of breaking that conscious routine by physically jumping into the pool must have appeared to my childish demeanor as an infringement on whatever traces of privacy the war had spared me.

The actual center within which the swimming pool was located was vast and boundless, much like the expansive promenade of cars that led to it. Just outside the pool, there was a food stall that sold burgers, hot dogs and fries to hungry ex-swimmers who now sit and overlook the waves of new swimmers take their place. The comfort of enjoying that food under the shade while witnessing the tumultuous waters just beyond you reminisces now of the familiar luxuries of the street corner with China Inn and al-Aqsa video game store, both of which also overlook an ocean of cars presumably overlooked by an ice cream store.

Backtracking towards the wide promenade of cars once again, I take us on a quintessential right turn just before we arrive at the pool. There, in this side street resided a destination which we frequented perhaps more than China Inn: a video rental store whose actual name escapes me and has instead disappeared under the guise of the store owner's first name, Zaki. Another person from my childhood whose last name enters a seclusion of forgetfulness, along with his store's name. Zaki is to be credited with introducing me to *Edward Scissorhands*, my first favorite film that welcomed me to Jordan, atop the mountain of Tariq.

Although I have forgotten the name of his store, I remember its architectural contours, as it existed at the time, just as well as I recall now his thick glasses, slender body and condensed smell of cigarettes. Zaki's store eloquently performed the eternal tango of all the greatest movies. It did this through a simple architectural motion. Since the space of the store was rather small, each of the walls were filled with movies and could be moved to the side to unveil even more films. Layers upon layers of films rested comfortably

235

behind one another like the endless depths of an ocean. Amidst all these sliding shelves there resided a still and silent mirror through which all visitors gazed, but only those of them who tasted the secret of films knew what they were witnessing.

This is the same movement animating my endless layers of interpretation that enchant the rough textures of old buildings, from Haifa street to Sweifiyya, into living characters fitting to replace forgotten human protagonists. Only by gazing at myself through the mirror at Zaki's store can I witness this act of translation from the past to the present, from architecture to human experience, from shelves filled with old movies with torn labels to events and people with half-forgotten names and faces.

Incidentally, all the movies I have inherited into my life from Zaki happen to linger on the side of fiction and fantasy. Whether it is *Edward Scissorhands*, *Hocus Pocus*, *Batman* or *Mortal Kombat*, these are iconic films that commemorate the 90's as much as they do the timeless creative healing that is born from the pain of separation and scattering of diaspora. Migrants resemble superheroes, like Batman, in the suffering they carry that sustains their movement towards equilibrium. However, they also emit an aura of foreignness and anxiety, like Edward, emanating from their native identity that has disintegrated into countless little fragments of cosmopolitan mockery.

The last site in Sweifiyya follows in the same footsteps of Zaki's video store, on a much grander scale. The American embassy in Amman, located just beyond this rental store, at least as it seems to my memory now, was a spectacle of a palace that barricaded itself within the gate of Zaki's gifts: the artistic effulgence from the West. The countless American movies and cartoons I had watched during my childhood in Jordan seem now like pamphlets, handed out by the American spirit, in preparation for my eventual long journey beyond the sea. This subtle and metaphoric marketing scheme was heightened in the last years prior to our departure from Jordan when I visited the embassy with my best friend from the mountain of Tariq, 'Adi, who took me to watch *Around the World in 80 Days*, amidst an ocean of Americans, in the heart of the diplomatic structure.

There could not be, perhaps, a more fitting movie to watch by a young Iraqi migrant whose temporary childhood in Jordan towards America is signaling its demise in the heart of an architectural *barzakh*, isthmus, between East and West. Sitting in the medium-sized theater room, surrounded by blond haired, white skinned and blue eyed Americans of all ages, I was physically overwhelmed by an ethnicity I had never experienced beforehand. Spiritually, however, I was merely witnessing a foretelling of impending changes and a subsistent lifestyle. For nothing embodies the fickle turmoils of diaspora like an embassy. In its glorious stature, it presents a confidence that obliterates any trace of anxiety. Inwardly, on the other hand, there lingers a trace of tradition succumbing to the pain of countless external and foreign forces. Together, tradition and change are made to witness the fleeting breaths of time in 80 days of destiny. While tradition attempts to process each of these days like an immortal civilization, the whispers of change simply laugh throughout the entire affair at the inevitable, privately-owned entertainment.

The second time I visit the embassy would be in a treacherous excitement longing to leave Jordan. Then, I once again had a foreign encounter with a consul who decorated our journey to the New World with due congratulations. It was only a few months later and thousands of miles farther that I would return to the ocean of foreign ethnicities and different colors. Then, with the solemn passing of time, the colors and ethnicities inverted. Now, it is the Arab faces, bodies and mannerisms that seem estranged to my imagination. They reside distantly and are made foreign by an aura of nostalgia. As we both sit still to contemplate the reel of the journey highlighted in the words and chapters of this book, the faces and bodies surrounding my trace of tradition cannot afford to laugh or regard my life as entertainment. Instead, they have succumbed to faded features or lost identities and names.

A Children's Dream in Shmeisani

Our next location in the final tour of Jordanian memories takes us to Shmeisani, a large section of Amman that, at the time, existed as a *barzakh*, or convergence between the mountain of Husayn's ancient ambiance and Sweifiyya's dress of pure modernity. From the first wing, Shmeisani received the inheritance of endless busy-ness and tightly embracing restaurants, stores and the ever-increasing city life. From the second wing, this dear place to my heart received an aura of youthfulness and a subtle gaze towards the future.

This last spiritual dress specifically emanated in two living entities which resided at the heart of Shmeisani and also in the center of my imagination until today. Both of them espoused the interests which school children cherished at the time and they each sought to direct the endless imagination of a youth, without limits, to their ambitions differently: one provided endless windows into the virtual world of video games and mythological contentions that externalize the countless tensions flooding children of the 90's. The second, on the other hand, tried to turn the entire ambiance of its body into renditions of a child's imagination that have been dressed in a physical and tangible garment.

Gardens of King 'Abdullah I welcome me again now for one last visit in its vast promenades and jostling spaces of arcades ornamented by restaurants and other forms of entertainment. Serendipitously, its genealogical attribution to the premier king harmonizes its existence in my heart now as the first memory alongside the second, awaited, place of exploration. Architecturally, this large park had as a most noticeable imprint the very spatial fingerprint that ties together the spirit of my past's narrative: vast and endless swathes of a white courtyard. Like a generous and hospitable canvas, the basin of these Gardens hosted an everlasting stream of colors that were painted by divine grace in forms of human visitors and the virtual characters that complemented their existence.

One could even say that the family of arcade machines which congregated warmly together in adjacent rooms, as ornaments on each side of the promenades, were themselves park-like enclosures for their virtual residents, mostly consisting of Mortal Kombat characters. Each of these heroes and villains engaged in countless bloody bouts of fatalities, brutalities and friendships that not only moved to life through the direct command of a young human child, but more importantly actually brought to life the internal fatalities, brutalities and friendships that lingered in hearts. It is not necessarily difficult to contemplate this ephemeral significance of video games by oneself, but it is certainly easier to taste it at a much larger scale as it existed in the Gardens of King 'Abdullah I and augmented now in lustrous symbolic power in my imagination.

This signifier is animated single handedly by the white courtyard undergirding and carrying the entire movement of the park. It is this auspicious spatial purity that also tethers this entertainment hub to the religious conclave of the mosque atop the mountain of

Tariq, in the presence of imagination which is the only host capable of deciphering a singular metaphysical codex from such drastically different ambiances; thereby rendering it a language through which they may engage in a conversation about the ineffable reality of existence and how it emanates in a myriad of entities foreign to all but their own selves.

Like many of the places I lived in, frequented and mentioned in this journal, this kingly Garden also swayed to the left and right, leaving hidden treasures just beyond the eyesight of the visitor. The vast expanse of the promenade and countless alcoves, each of which is filled with numerous siblings of arcade machines, now bewilders my memory and overwhelms any ability to distinguish what lay beyond these mysterious right and left turns. I merely remember a left arm extending the promenade towards the west of its own northerly direction. And then, there emerges nothing in my heart's eye save an abundance of parking spots and one particular store that holds a special place in my heart.

This is a donut shop that now appears to me as a branch of Dunkin Donuts somewhere at the end of the park. Although, it most likely was not an actual clone of the famed American dessert shop, this harmony is born from the symbolism that donuts had for a migrant child in Jordan who had only heard of America from his family and sought to find the traces of the New World wherever he could spare them. In this case, any donuts sufficed as an emblem of the mythically glorious Dunkin Donuts.

I also find myself now in the vicinity of this shop and embraced within its cozy arms during the stygian Jordanian nights. If we remember, it was these same nights that still haunt me with their beauty, as I laid in my bedroom, atop the mountain of Husayn. The flood of feelings, channeling themselves to me through the bedroom window that embraced my bed, and which gradually revealed themselves to me through the decades, reappear now inside this shop. Just as the window in my bedroom was a gate into another dimension of imaginal reflections, so does the inside of this shop, its architectural nuances and unique smell augment themselves now to be august renditions of that same imaginal presence.

There was a surreal silence in this shop, even when the night was young. Whereas the alcoves of the arcade machines, in the heart of the park, were filled with the murmurs of people, this store stood like a serene observer from a far. The solitude of the seller standing by himself in the outskirts of the kingly Garden foretold of a dessert that he sold which was enveloped by the energy of the moment, such that they emerged as priceless metaphors for the sweetness of reflective knowledge.

The lighting of the shop, emanating from an ambitious neon light, turned the inside of this dessert land into an overwhelming light-filled space. Then, when coupled with the darkness of the night, it seemed like the full moon itself had descended in the middle of the kingly Garden in order to serenade the people with unforeseen delicacies from just beyond the sea of reality. It is in this way, and at this special moment, while I write these memories to share with you and me, that this donut shop on the outskirts of the Gardens of King 'Abdullah I unites with the window in my bedroom atop the mountain of Husayn. The distant exotic wonders of the full moon, residing across the horizons of my bedroom, come close now, embodied in the form of this shop. The sweetness of the donuts and their cold touch to the tongue seem like a very fitting performance of the cold vestiges of empty space where the full moon resides in its glory.

Also residing within the inner movement of Shmeisani is the second heartbeat of children; a place where imagination ruled and molded the very physical contours of the ambiance, a movement which it still executes successfully in my imagination. Princess Haya's Cultural Center was much smaller in its physical size than the Gardens of King 'Abdullah I, a shortcoming for which it compensated with a larger diversity in the land of imagination. In contrast to the singular family of arcade machines that ornamented the alcoves of the Garden, the hidden caves of the Cultural Center hosted entire tribes of activities, each of which satisfied the inquisitive spirit of children at any given moment, and consistently renewed their captivating forms day after day.

The exact time and frequency of my excursions at this Center fade now under the overwhelming weight of timelessness that surround all the memories from my past during their convalescence in the land of imagination. Nevertheless, I do remember that I spent most of time there during the summers, when my normal schooling at Deir al-Latin and Terra Sancta was exchanged for a plethora of creative delicacies with friends. These activities also extended the creative reach of the Center beyond its architectural boundaries to the extremities of Amman, just as the Donut shop and arcade machines situated me at the very boundaries of virtual and physical spaces.

Right outside the Center's humble gate there stood a bank for Children. My father had deposited a few dollars while I was still living in Jordan that remained until later, when I had moved to America. By then, the few dollars had grown to hundreds in a harmonious movement to my growth and distance away from

248

home. Its lingering presence in Jordan also eloquently performs my own conscience which still resides there, frozen not only within the dimensions of space and geography that one can return to, but also a time period that cannot be met again. Of course, my happiness when I received the money from that bank emerged from my futile unawareness of the significance of that wealth's own migration, following me, from Jordan all the way to America. With this final piece of belonging that had also entered the movement of diaspora, I could only rely upon my attachments in the imagination thenceforth; the physical and temporal embrace had been entirely severed.

The towering entrance of the kingly Garden also contrasted with the unassuming entrance of the Center. Like most residences in my life, the Center also marketed its breeze of hospitality at the immediate threshold of the entrance. A hamburger restaurant delivered a constant stream of these delicious smells to both the intrigued passersby outside and immersed children inside the Center's embrace. During the days I wandered around the corners of this small land, I was as infatuated with consuming a burger from this restaurant as I was with admitting the floods of simple realizations into my heart and mind from the various caves inside.

It is these practically endless niches of Princess Haya Cultural Center that overwhelm my journey now into the past with a flood of emotions, meetings and incidents. Complementing the restaurant's sweet smells, immediately to the right of the entrance is a planetarium that espouses a breeze in the realm of sound and music. These vibrations were of the planets and stars that were housed deep within the planetarium. However, these renditions from space were muffled behind a rhythmic pattern of Pac Man and Galactica emanating from computers that ornamented the lobby of the planetarium and which were frequented by more children than the vicinities of space that had been brought near, inside the very boundaries of the Center.

The specific moments I spent inside this planetarium dissipate now, perhaps due to the overwhelming expanse of the Center which also demands our attention. Aside from a few fleeting blinks drawing my attentive indulgence in Pac Man and Galactica or witnessing a rendition of our solar system in the ceiling of the planetarium, my attention is drawn elsewhere. Continuing deeper towards the heart of the Center, away from the entrance, we are met with a sibling in science that embraces the inner walls of the planetarium. This humble museum performed its close kinship to the planetarium by having a singular outer wall tying both cultural caves together in an eternal marriage; notwithstanding the differences they exhibited inwardly.

In contrast to the cozy and tight contours of the planetarium and its lobby ornamented with computers from the 90's, the science museum furnished visitors with an expansive showcase of a wide array of physical phenomena that have withstood the withering effects of countless centuries. Touring the entire museum in a circular motion returns you to your same position within only a few steps. This sudden completion, alongside the wide-ranging demonstrations you witness, from volcanoes to lifting mechanisms, seems to be a fitting symbolism for the dream-like spectacle of human life, which we have ventured through in these pages; for it also seems to be a series of timelessness explorations of a singular meaning from infinite perspectives; much like the resilient prism of my science fair project at Terra Sancta college.

Although the science museum and planetarium were siblings in science, they contended in more than just their spatial limits. Rather, there was another architectural performance through which the museum sought to differentiate itself from its smaller brother. The hidden quarters of the star showcase, residing behind a lobby of entertainment machines sporting Pac Man and Galactica, contrast with the large glass windows that fully revealed the inner workings of the museum to outsiders. I shudder to suppose that these architectural differences are haphazard, although they may appear that way when separated from the inner workings of both caves. Without a doubt, the planetarium reveals its imaginal self to me now as a virginal bashful sister that secluded herself behind a ruse of a pearl necklace consisting of white computers, while her sibling, the science museum, fully flouted his masculinity through the glass windows that showcased the wide muscular array of endless experiments.

And yet, this outward hierarchy, setting apart the feeble sister from the strong brother, alludes to an inverse reality that resides hidden behind this illusive architecture: the showcase of physical spectacle that the museum displayed in full grandeur crumbles before the more luxurious whispers of stars and planets that protected themselves behind a veil of femininity and virtual entertainment. Of course, beyond these twin layers of architectural distinctions and tangible separations there still resides the more precious theophany speaking through these preceding paragraphs: masculinity and femininity reveal themselves consistently in a similar manner to this shared performance between the planetarium and science museum. Between gendered human forms, distinguished souls and performative quarters, femininity remains the subtlest ruse to the rose at the end of one's path.

Connecting the entrance of the museum and that of the next cave of creativity in the Center, and also sheltering the path in-between from the soaring Jordanian sun, is pillared walkway that reminisces of the liminal architectural interstice in Terra Sancta that helped students transition from the life of the courtyard to the inner sanctum of the school's hallways and classrooms. In reality, however, this sheltered walkway at the heart of the Center was an interstice at the threshold of not only two, but three hidden caves, each of which housed worlds and dimensions of activities.

Like the heart itself, from this sheltered walkway also emerged the various arteries and branches of the Center in all cardinal directions. Immediately facing the museum was the children's library and T.V. room. In many ways, the hemisphere of the Center brought together through its architectural design and ambiance the two earlier siblings: the planetarium and science museum. The inner sanctum of this third synthesizing space, with its tightly rounded global shape, resembled the planetarium's embodiment of earth's curvature as it gazes into distant space. Meanwhile, the outer rim of this room paid homage to the rings of Saturn, in this case orbiting and protecting the globe-like seating area in the middle and resembling the circumambulatory motion guiding tourists around the contours of the museum that resided just across the shaded walkway.

If that is the architectural analogy tethering the planetarium, museum and this third cave in yet another kinship, then the distinct ambiance of each quarter in this last area reveals the spiritual root of this similarity. On the one hand, the tightly-rounded seating area in the center, resembling the planetarium, also marketed the affairs of technology through a large television that broadcast endless cartoons for children to watch. Meanwhile, the outer-rim consisted of countless books that documented the annals of natural history which the museum performed in visual excellence around the clock.

Altogether, the color schemes of these three caves further augmented their distinct roles in the Center. The white atmosphere of the lobby in the planetarium, which was divided between the hues of the computer machines and walls, contrasted with its inner sanctum that wore the dress of stygian darkness in order to convey the abyssal distance of space. In-between this opposition of colors, all children my age at the Center comprehended solemnly the distinction between the physical and spiritual worlds without words or explanations.

Meanwhile, the museum paid homage to the subtle details of earth's soil and the countless miracles that occur within it in the vivid browns manifesting in the models of volcanos, rocks and metals that filled the ether of the round hall. This color choice does not seem to be haphazard, at least when coupled with the ceaseless movement of the experiments which the hue dressed: it was a testimony that this particular shade contained the secret spirit which caused the machinations of the earth to give forth life during every breath and blink.

Lastly, the library and T.V. room distinguished itself from the neighboring caves through the calmer family of blue tints that covered the corners of the round room. Like a journey towards a center of increasing vivid experiences, the lighter heavenly-blue shade of the outer rim ring of bookshelves simultaneously granted their young readers the serenity to enjoy their books in peace and foretold of a more intense engagement with this color in the central globe surrounding the television of childhood. There, both the seating area and carpet ostentatiously proclaimed the strongest tint of blues, reminiscing of unforeseen ocean depths and symbolizing the endless stream of cartoons that filled the ambiance of this inner conclave.

This cave was connected to another sibling, much like the planetarium shared an outer wall with the museum, that channeled a creative aura similar to reading the annals of natural history next door. Here however, we also witness a shift in the energy of the caves towards this wing of the Center. The scientific and cosmic frontiers that met us at the entrance give way to more artistic inclinations, beginning with the ring of reading materials in the library room.

This cave next door transitions us to the art studio. I recognize now that I barely spent any time in this room, save a few instances that, perhaps, were merely intended as memoirs for this journal. Either way, all I remember is that the ambiance of the room returns us to the brownish hues of the museum, which can be clearly seen from the windows across the sheltered walkway.

However, the brown color that dressed the art studio does not have the same spirit as the similar form that occupied the models of volcanos and rocks in the scientific showcase. Rather, the earthy tints here represented the organic fragrance of wooden worktables that filled the room. The countless paintings born from the studio left their traces in a kaleidoscope of colors on the wooden surfaces and appeared like a visual rendition of the Center's contribution through the decades.

The caves housing the library and art studio steer us in a circular fashion back towards the museum, forming a courtyard of, unsurprisingly, white marble that reminisces of the courtyard of generosity in Terra Sancta, together with the sheltered walkway that also pays homage to the pillared interstice in that school, and that singular motif which tethers the Center to the mosque atop the mountain of Tariq and strip mall next to our white palace in Haifa street.

The last cave that perfects the curved character of the courtyard and connects the art studio to the museum is itself the perfect artistic addition to the repertoire of activities available at the Center. The theater found here was in many ways, at least to me, a delicacy rarely enjoyed by children of the Center. I recall only one instant when I volunteered to participate in a musical performance about marital heartbreak, carried out by underage children. Although I did not play the role of a troubled spouse, I did perform the equally ironic task of pretending to be a judge who foresaw the endless books of complaints from other children his age, pretending to be quarreling married couples, and then issued a verdict of truth in a world of make-belief circumstances.

Let us transition to the final two caves at the Center. The first of these, in closest proximity to the creative shore of libraries, art studios and theaters is an outdoor play area filled with sand that foretold of a nearby imaginary seashore. countless children climbed swings and ladders to expend energy for which they could not find a place to place within the other enclosed creative vortices at the Center.

I solemnly admit now that I did not spend much time in this play either, except a few instances which I can count on my fingers. Unlike other places and people mentioned in this journal about which I have also remarked that I recollect only mere traces, I'm certain that my ephemeral imaginary presence in this area is not due to distant memories, but rather my own physical resistance to such arenas that encourage entertaining movements. Not to mention that I would always set in motion a diasporic narrative of my own childish energy across the spectrum of all the caves before even arriving in this arena with imaginary sandy shores. Endless pieces of me, of a much younger me, have become part of the ether of the Center's other caves and its own younger apparition.

And yet, my physical body's divorce from this play area contrasts with its quintessential presence in my memory now. Just as those friends whose faces and names my body and mind recollected better than its own self, at one point in time, now escape me except for a few traces, this arena finds itself in an opposing condition. The dearth of its physical presence hearkens for an imaginary compensation to satisfy its role in shaping and completing my journey. This is yet another perplexing eccentricity of the marriage between memory and imagination. Those things we loved most in body we sometimes forget most, in order to long for them most; while those things we barely engaged in our bodily forms become constant living spirits that sustain that longing and allow it to thrive.

That central purpose of this arena no doubt resides in the wavy sand that turned the entire play area into a gentle desert for the children of the Center. In its kindness, this sand also carried that more important spirit of the open ended ocean that perhaps escaped me then, but definitely visits me now. What is memory, imagination, the past, distance, nostalgia and all their siblings but an endless ocean upon whose shore we are strolling endlessly, reminiscing over colors, smells, textures and smiles along the way! Most importantly, we are also treating ourselves to the child-like freedom of engaging with these sensory forms like my generation treated the swings in that play area two decades ago.

It is perhaps not a coincidence, then, that next to the play area, also outside the other caves of the Center, there stood tall, for a few months, a special exhibit commemorating the ancient past of dinosaurs, their various species and exotic sounds which filled the either of the Center and could even be heard all the way at the entrance. At that moment in my history when they erected that monument, I had already watched Steven Spielberg's monumental Jurassic Park countless times. Witnessing models of those dinosaurs, up close and personal, was a nostalgic journey with two streams: a sojourn within the Hollywood of pomp and circumstance that resided across thousands of miles in the New World and another, some countless years beforehand, at a time when these larger than life, now imaginary and mythic, creatures filled the earth.

The last cave at the Center performed its cardinal rank in the sequence of creative springs, which we have discussed thus far in this chapter, by residing at the far end of this children's imaginarium. This was not a cave that had obtained an official recognition from the other caves nor the administration of the Center for that matter. Rather, it was an empty space which could and was used for a variety of purposes. It is in this ambivalent capacity that this space at a distant gained more imaginal power than even the library with its endless stream of books and cartoons, art studio with wooden tables laden with a colorful history or the theater whose stage testified to the thespian abilities of countless Jordanian children.

Of course, this imaginal power only emerges once we can offer the physical forms of such spaces a eulogy of post-mortem, after which their spirits are freed from the prisons of time and walls of dimensionality. It is in this seventh sense that this last cave at a distant in the Center of Princess Haya now becomes freed of its physical distance and lack of official recognition to become the only vortex at the Center that has been granted this power of ambivalence and carries within its shifting transparent walls oceans of memories from within and without the Center.

This unique imaginal power is augmented by the fact that my visits to this distant periphery of the center occurred also at times separated from those moments during which I surrounded myself with the auras of the other caves. As a matter of fact, the entire Center had closed its eye lids of activity and movement by the time the small group of children, myself included, returned to its vicinity for a faint trace of life at the far end of this vast complex. We even performed this distinction in time and place by donning white clothing that carried an aura of tradition and ritual transcending hundreds of years. The only change in color in these textured perfumes of the outer body were colored belts that allude to journeys across ranks and stations spanning an equal number of decades and centuries.

This is the manner in which our weekly march to Tae-Kwon-Do training took place then and still does now in the white courtyard of my imagination. The ambivalent aura of the space within which this practice took place appears clearly now as it brings together scattered and diasporic fragments into the native abode of homeliness. For it is in the original embrace of the neighborhood of Husayn that I was first introduced to this martial art form. It was there, as well, that I experienced the tumultuous desire to leave the way this art was rigidly crafted. The powerful strands of ambivalence in this last cave at the Center, however, dictated that I discover later a certain union between the two ritual centers: the second teacher, from Shmeisani, was the guide of the first, from the mountain of Husayn.

There is one particular incident which captures both the ambivalence of this last momentary cave and the perplexing power of destiny that forces the mind and reason to submit to a hunger of imagination. My friend Tamer, whom we have already met in Gardens street, appeared first in my life at the juncture of this periphery of the Center and reaches us now from across the distance of Amman. As I stood there with him one day, before practice, I saw my first Tae-Kwon-Do teacher sitting and weeping next to his and my new teacher. He lamented losing an important competition and simply sat, awaiting comfort from his teacher … all he needed was a gentle reminder that the spirit of his craft lingered beyond competitions, victories or defeats. It resided in longing to witness the spiritual and creative epics dormant within each movement of an art like Tae-Kwon-Do and the mythic legends to which these motions incessantly pay homage.

Between Twin Palaces

Our final march in Amman takes place in this chapter, at the threshold of two friendly familial palaces that belong to friends who opened their physical, spiritual and the architectural arms of their vast homes to accept my family into their equally expansive hospitable hearts. I have chosen to situate the memories of these homes together and at the end of this journey not because they belong in a single embrace or because I spent brief moments there at the end of my physical residence in Amman. Rather, I present them here and now because they share an imaginal reality that renders them similar anomalies among the annals of memorable forms from the past.

This common trait hearkens to those half-forgotten friends whose young faces are the only traces I remember now, amidst the faded apparitions of their lost names. These two familiar palaces have also lost their genealogies and exact locations in Amman. The only remaining truth to their existence is the ghost of their form in my memory which recurrently visits me every now and then as one of the countless safe harbors from a past illumined by the innocence of childhood. Their lost genealogies are the result of my forgetfulness which has caused their exact location in Amman to be an ambivalence obfuscating all my organs. They emerge now architectural orphans, having lost their parents, the neighborhood and street which housed them, to the war which the procession of time declares against the present moment as it marches towards its final demise.

The first of these palaces belonged to an Egyptian family, somewhere at the outskirts of Amman. While I still remember the faces of the husband, wife and sons, the only traces left of their names are the elder woman's first name, Suhair. This name, married to the Arabic word *sahra*, a nightly conclave among friends, lessens the loss felt by the absent names of the other family members. Its polysemous nature grants it a special strength to carry the burdens of morning well into the most stygian corners of the night. Here, we find another advantage and serendipity in the harmony between the name of the lady of the house, nightly conversations, her forgotten family and the magic of nighttime: The family of colors that granted the interior of the house its warmth and serenity attracted that energy antithetical to the light of day. The vivid red hues which filled the walls of the dining room, mixed with lush greens and earthly browns relieve my imagination now of any traces of my presence in that abode prior to the sun's slumber.

That is only partially due to the fact that we rarely visited Suhair's house during the daytime. The more significant reason emerges in the harmony between this historical fact and this lady's name; a symbiosis which etched the memorialized faces of all her family members within the contours of her name and all that it carries of nightly meanings and meetings. As expected from the previous analogies and harmonies discussed in this journey, it is hardly surprising that I would try to present you, dear reader, with such outlandish connections between the forgetfulness of memory, Arabic names, places and the space where they all meet and converse in love.

We have experienced the diversity of hospitalities in these different residences and how each abode channels its generosity in a unique form that greets each visitor as soon as their gaze embraces the interior of these houses, whether it is the guest room or vast and expansive windows that open the sight of the architectural space into the insight of Amman's spiritual zephyrs. In the case of Suhair's house, what immediately meets the eye is an unusual area of transition that prepares you and I for the drastic change in colors and ambiances from the simplicity of the neighborhood's roads to the sophisticated artisanship enveloping the interior.

As we march from the front door, which fades into forgetfulness now, through this interstice towards its demise and the beginning of the actual house, you can feel the sun's influence dwindling and its illumination gradually giving way to more artificial sources of glow and glory. That sun, which still hosts my memories, and countless others, in the classrooms of Terra Sancta, artistically abdicated its throne here and granted this power to collect and embrace memories to the melancholic eternity of night. This seems to be an exchange required by the power of Suhair's name, which alludes to the governance of nightly conversations.

And so, just as my memories in this house linger on the side of nightly visitations, so does every atom of the house itself also come to life through the gazes of the night and its full moon in all its glory. Ironically, the marriage between this vast palace and nightliness did not procure the coldness of emptiness as an aura that surrounds the interior. Rather, there was an indelible warmth that surrounded you wherever your gazes looked and intended to go. This was undoubtedly the result of intense emotions and the lingering breaths of timeless conversations between the myriad of colors that dressed the walls of the house.

As I recall the palace back into my insight's purview now, it seems as though every room espoused at least one wall that bore the imprint of redness. Thenceforth, that specific face constructed unique friendships with the other walls and colors of its room that differed from those other chambers in the palace. Altogether, the ambiance of each private quarter differed from the other yet formed an indispensable component of a larger family history of colors and the mundane details of their lives and stories.

Returning to the front threshold of the house, which meets us immediately following the interstitial veranda, we find a dining room that seems to linger in darkness, rarely used by the hosts, at least while they're in the company of friends. In this way, this dining room resembles the secluded imprint found in the dining room of my aunt's house in Ghadir, which also resided in a subtle darkness, save for a television that set that attests to countless showings of *Terminator 2* with family and relatives. Like that humble dinner hall across an ocean of sand, this nightly abode of Suhair also contributed, perhaps unintentionally, to this isolation of the dinner table and its surrounding ambiance by situating it next to the guest room which exercised an indomitable monopoly in entertaining and serving visitors.

And so, perhaps, the only purpose which this dining room did serve is as a symbol of hospitality. Like pretentious plastic flowers in an eager vase, this empty room sought to merely allude to the hospitable spirit of the hosts. It was an architectural representation of a human hand's welcoming gesture divorced from the scent of food and its taste. The dining room points towards the guest room which was the right wing of the veranda that welcomes us into the house.

Whatever the dining room lacked in life, the guestroom in this palace of Suhair compensated for and alleviated in an abundance of nightly conversations. The absence of light which filled the surroundings of the dinner table and its family of chairs is met with a humble recognition from the guest room windows that admitted into the seating area the quaint moonlight of Jordanian nights. Likewise, the burden of loneliness carried emptily by the family of dining chairs is alleviated by lofty sofas whose memory now projects traces of smiling faces emerging from those nightly conversations.

The guest room's homage towards the forsaken dining room does not end here. For across the horizon from the sofas of nightly conversations appears a doorway that provides a glimpse into a vast kitchen that resembles the Parisian cuisines which take us back to the primordial kitchen in our white palace in Haifa street. Although I never spent anytime in this cooking quarter of Suhair's palace, its importance now transcends my physical presence within its boundaries. It emerges as a pivotal component in the guest room's intricate scheme to pay tribute to its neighboring deserted dining room. Mixed with the nightly moonlight and conversations, the gaze towards the kitchen completes the requirements needed for a spiritual dining life to emerge in this part of the house despite the apparent physical death of such a common festival.

The aura of this kitchen, with its overwhelming spaciousness, apparently needed to overflow into more than one quarter of nightly conversations, and so it did into a secondary family room immediately adjacent to this cooking quarter. In contrast to the previous vast guest room, this distant extension was a much smaller alcove that merely helped carry any private breaths between friends, over from the guest room, into a more intimate setting. The humbleness of the seating area in this section of the palace reminisces more of the equally modest home of our Christian friends in Baghdad than any of the houses we have encountered so far in Jordan. However, it is doubtful that the small size of the room is the only factor that contributes to this imaginary similarity. More likely, it is the nightly ambiance that ornaments the existence of both these architectural spaces in my memory.

Just like the moonlight that illuminated the guest room and similar stygian hues that filled the Iraqi Christian abode with life, so does this small family room also thrive through windows that incline towards nighttime colors and breezes. Like the guest room, the warm brown and olive hues ornamenting the walls and furniture sustain a separated imagination with enough motivation to revisit such palaces and distinguish clearly between the sunlight of day and moonlight of night amidst an otherwise tumultuous ocean of overlapping shades of fade and fate.

The boundary of the palace in my memory extends only a little bit further, around the corner to the room of one of Suhair's sons. There, a younger me was shown an abundance of hospitality by a reserved young man who was much younger than my current self. My maturity now is able to indulge and appreciate that kindness shown at the time. For his age, he showed much more elegance than his age required or permitted. The insanity of teenagers in the 90's was somehow humbled and balanced in his disposition and he allowed me to spend countless hours with his video games.

My equally endless focus on those forms of entertainment has rendered all other physical aspects of the room obsolete for the imagination. The only thing remaining of this part of the house, and any extension of it thereof, are just pixelated fragments of Michael Jackson's *Moonwalker* and Indiana Jones' *Temple of Doom* on Sega Genesis, both of which are masterpieces that attest to that period's cultural spirit as much as my own childhood and time in this palace. Within a very small television set, one similar to countless other ones that I had in all my Jordanian and Iraqi homes, I was able to undertake mythic journeys into the Wild West … preemptively rearing my soul for the imminent transition. Except, in this case, the very theater and stage upon which these timeless sojourns took place have themselves become part of the myth in memory, all thanks to the journey of this journal.

I leave Suhair's palace with the satisfaction of giving its traces and colors their due remembrance. This so we can transition the second-to-last architectural breath in this book. This appears in the form of another palace that moved its arms to embrace its guests in an impeccable imitation of its owners, one of whom, their son, is one of my dearest friends, Suleiman. The clarity with which Suhair's lavish home presents itself again to me, at least from the interstitial veranda until her son's bedroom, contrasts with the enigma surrounding Suleiman's even more extravagant house. This is hardly because I simply do not remember it very well, but rather due to the altar of his residence which appears like a spirit divided into two bodies, each of which sheltered him and his family for a while, as I witnessed this entire affair of transition.

I first met Suleiman at Terra Sancta. The brief amount of time I spent at that school should conjure images of an equally short-lived friendship. However, a show of gratitude is due to video games that brought us together during those couple of years and stretched them to match the warped timeline of virtual temporality. Just as we were able to traverse an entire lifetime in pixels within the span of a few days or weeks, so were entire oceans of conversations and personal growth in a friendly mirror harmoniously folded within those last, fleeting, couple of years that I spent in Jordan. Meanwhile, my role as the friend who witnessed his transition between palatial abodes seems now eerily reminiscent of our school's liminal courtyard, which helped students similarly transition from the expansiveness of a child's play into the reserved hallways of studious education.

As far as I can remember now, I have been to each house only once. A singular taste that suffices for a memorable remembrance for each expansive abode. This soliloquy is made even more vivid by the fact that the architectural ambiance of each home embraces countless other residences we have discussed during this journey in threads of texture and color. It is only now, decades later, that I begin to witness these twin palaces of a friend to be essentially different forms, in an endless procession, that collapse in an abyss of two essential meanings: an aging immortal tradition and ever-newly born modernity.

Once we are able to witness these two family homes of Suleiman through this prism, of tradition and modernity, then the transition which his family made from the first to second house becomes a seamless and natural transition from one wave of time to another. For it was the final breaths of that first house, a bastion of old age that pays homage to my grandparents' ancient castle in Karrada or our Iraqi friends' second abode in Amman, amidst the guardians or greenery, that welcomed me into its arms immediately prior to bidding myself and its family farewell towards their new, much more expansive and young, abode and equally fledgling neighborhood of Gardens.

The only thing I remember from that first house are these aging walls. The inner chamber wherein lay the bedrooms and living room was akin to a triage lobby at a local hospital that faces countless rooms of patients in convalescence. In this case, the bedrooms where not for patients, but rather the family members were themselves the doctors who were gazing upon the house in mercy, as it transitions towards the death of their companionship and perhaps another chapter in its faded life.

The humble shades of the walls and rooms supported this inevitable transition. Altogether, it seemed as though all the furniture had dressed itself in the house's favorite color, varying tints of browns, as a show of support for its resistance against a terminal sickness known as diaspora and desertion. This color was chosen, it seems, due to its own old age that beckons for the ancient soil of the earth. Through their collective dress rehearsal in this color, both the house and furniture were performing this primordial beginning and ultimate end of all things: to return to earth. This seems like a rather grandiose lesson; one that is, nevertheless, indispensable enough to tether and attach itself to as mundane an action as moving from one house to another.

In this way, the furniture of Suleiman's first house inherited the walls' ability to age regally. They perfumed the distinct brown shades of each member of the furniture family, including pillows, mattresses and tables in a special fragrance of warmth and homeliness strong enough to captivate the memory and imagination of a migrant Iraqi child in diaspora. As we transitioned from one room to the next, where Suleiman's video games resided, I witnessed a slight change in colors involving the introduction of white blankets and bedsheets that stood out laboriously in this overwhelming brown atmosphere; an abnormality resembling the contention between the modern youth of those video games and that home's ancient gaze which found foreign all things virtual and pixelated.

This creative contention takes us to Suleiman's second palatial home, somewhere else in Amman which also eludes me now. It is wondrous, that these two homes are orphans deprived of the genealogy of neighborhoods and addresses save their own sibling-relationship and the historical trace of belonging to Suleiman's family. Even the modern and expansive ambiance with which this second home presents itself pays homage to the older and smaller sibling in a mirror of refraction as opposed to reflection: the rays of old age, humbleness and experience from the first house dissipate in a thousand directions that, together, transform into a mosaic of vibrancy, colorfulness and pride of youth.

Like the older sibling, I also remember only faint traces of this new house. However, together, the collage of these remembered quarters comes together for a singular imaginative house which housed Suleiman and his family. An abode that combines old age and youth, experience and pure naivete, wrinkled walls and smooth ones that have just seen the light of day. Indeed, these are paradoxical meetings and contradiction that fit harmoniously within the perplexing safe harbor of memory and imagination.

Whereas the bedrooms and their hospital-like lobby are what lingers within me from the first house, what appears now from the younger sibling is a flamboyant staircase, the likes of which you will only find in the enchanted palaces of fairy tales. This was a spiral that was expansive enough in size to house the entire family and lavish enough in color to don a dress of gold that covered the entire body of its handles. It also eerily reminisced of elaborate haunted mansions, the likes of which one could find in the celebrated video game from the 90's, *Resident Evil*. This probably explains why Suleiman and I reenacted famous scenes from this video game atop the staircase, switching roles between the protagonist hero and villainous zombies.

This was a reenactment of an ancient myth; one that many vessels had been able to capture before *Resident Evil*, including the subtle contention in colors and textures between Suleiman's twin homes of age and modernity. It is also the spirit of war animating a life of migration from destruction to survival and from the vestiges of a crushed home to another estranged land. It is also the withered ink of a journal attempting to discover the remnants of life within this constant transition that has been imprinted and embedded within diaspora. In this last case, our ancient myth emerges in a clash between past and present. However, imagination likes to insert various plot twists in its version of this myth. These appear as unannounced inversions between the hero and villain; not singular exchanges, but ones as constant and incessant as the waves of the ocean of reality. One moment the past ravages you while the present seeks your rescue. In another blink, the present poisons your feelings with desolate deprivation and the past heals you with nostalgia.

Unexpectedly, this new lavish home did not espouse a kitchen as expansive as the rest of the house. Rather, its cozy small size and brown hues, which resembled in their humbleness the bedrooms from the older home, seemed to direct attention away from the cooking quarters to other areas of the home as bastions of hospitality. And yet, it is this humble size of the kitchen which augments the hospitality of its owners. The large feasts which they lavished upon simple visitors, like myself, revealed their boundless generosity which must have been the true spiritual source and origin of the architectural expansiveness of their home.

The last remembered area of this house is an external protrusion that performs this expansiveness. This is a small building in the garden behind the house wherein Suleiman and his younger brothers kept all their toys, including the celebrated video games, for whose sake I regularly visited Suleiman. Just as these video games overwhelmed the details of the older house with their pixelated and virtual ambiance, so do they also turn the newly born walls in this young palace to faded memories that could barely keep themselves standing into life upon their feeble corners and hesitant textures. This also prudently describes the biography of my friendship with Suleiman which began in Terra Sancta and was destined to reach the tender age of two before the claws of diaspora takes me suddenly, once again, towards the unknown.

I remember spending time with Suleiman and another friend at a lavish Pizza Hut somewhere in one of the luxurious neighborhoods of Amman, akin to Sweifiyya. The exorbitant ambiance of this Jordanian Pizza Hut reflected both, Suleiman's palatial ancestry and the youthful birth of these Western restaurant chains that contrasted with their older siblings in America much like my friend's twin homes. This was a sudden and shocking realization I discovered when I finally saw the older sibling of Pizza Hut in the New World and discovered that it long since had taken its youthfulness and performed its own reverse pilgrimage to Jordan. This is its own diaspora, caused most probably by newly rising restaurants that forced Pizza Hut to vacate its age and pride.

We all went together later to watch *Air Force One*, an old movie now that was just released at the time. We saw, in a newly built theater, the extravagant escapades of presidential powers and triumphs in the New World. It was not a very different experience from witnessing the valiancy of the Western hero as portrayed in Indiana Jones, especially since Harrison Ford, who dons the outfit of Mr. Jones, the archaeology professor turned treasure hunter, also performs the role of the president who, like the actor's alter ego, also rescues priceless treasures against all odds. This convergence of Ford upon my life in two distinct forms was hardly a coincidence, any more than the tight embrace which the American embassy gave to Zaki's video store, between which I witnessed *Edward Scissorhands*, *Batman* and *Around the World in Eighty Days*, was not a happenstance .

I also remember that the last stygian moments during which I waited for my father to pick me from the front of the theater involved a farewell between myself and the shadows of my friends. The next day, I would be visiting the New World for the first time. The only lingering thread of hope, at the time, tethering me to Amman was the video game *Tomb Raider 2*, which I had just bought and began to play. Its enigmatic and unknown plot was an abyss waiting to unfold like my unknown future ... and it remains in that condition since then. The next, and last, time I would see Suleiman was during a brief visit to Jordan after migration. At our last apartment in Gardens, Suleiman brought his PlayStation One for us to play together. Unfortunately, he assumed that I had brought the controllers with me. He did not know that like my spiritual self, I was now divided between East and West. Like the decapitated birds that transported me from Iraq to Jordan, I had to also leave a part of me across the sea; to establish an identity and create yet another place in a foreign space. And so, we did not play video games that day. Rather, we were satisfied gazing into friendly eyes that were destined to grow gradually estranged from one another for decades, until the present moment.

Interlude

And so, we depart Amman, heading towards the unknown, eventually being delivered to the safety of the 'New World'. On the way to the airport, we are met with one last trace of childhood that fits the profile of extravagant, ancient, spacious and hospitable places that have hosted us throughout the journey of this book. This is a timeless castle residing in the middle of the desert that has, nevertheless, received the breezes of generosity from both Jordan and Iraq and hosted my family and younger self countless times during the celebrated 90's.

Kan Zaman, or 'Once Upon a Time', is the name given to this Roman castle which resided on the way to the airport and had been transformed into a family-friendly tourist attraction with restaurants, coffee shops and specialty boutiques. Its name harmonizes nicely with its history, both of which, in turn, help this castle transcend the boundaries of time and place to represent now one last remnant of my Middle Eastern identity. As a Roman-built bastion of power, it positions its territory not only in Jordan, but also Iraq, through those countless wars which the Byzantines unleashed against the Persians who ruled the land between the two rivers. This liminal temporality finds itself now translated into a geography at the threshold, between city and desolate desert, land and air, soil and sea, home and diaspora.

It is indeed the perfect location for a migrant-in-diaspora to visit incessantly. The luxurious restaurants, coffee shops and specialty boutiques reminisce of the duty free quarters found at airports and that intend to make travelers feel a semblance of stability in an interlude between their traversal of endless miles. Then, the enormous bricks in aging brown hues that meet your eye, outside and inside, further augment your sense of movement as they dissipate your sense of history and civilization. Each of these bricks carries between their crevices the soul of ancient Rome and yet is coerced to gaze upon a youthful generation who has forced the ancient ambiance of this place into submission for the purposes of luxury and familial entertainment.

Although the actual entrance of this castle evades me now, I somehow remember that, at a distance, we depart from the main highway and turn in such a magical way that we then go under the highway again, marching towards the castle which appears in the distance in all its glory. Such a swerving detour is not at all surprising. After all, the spirit and secret of Kan Zaman also resides just beneath the surface of its ancient bricks. Under the timeless age of each stone are those eternal gazes of experience and civilization.

Turning right at the main gate, we are met by the coffeeshops and restaurants that are filled with an endless stream of people who bring the ancient castle to life and remind of a memory from a distant past. Undoubtedly, the eyes of the bricks that have witnessed countless generations of visitors is more well aware of fashion and the dress code of dissipating time. It also gazes with a humbled and solemn awareness at the absent-mindedness of people in a generation which veils them from contemplating their looming transition to memory, like a single body, in order to give way to new generations, with new fashions and ambitions.

Ironically, sitting in these lavish restaurants from ancient times, I overheard singers and bands intimate Arab folklore from a not-so-distant past. The Iraqi song *Foug al-Nakhal*, above the palm tree, rings now in my mind as a migrant song that, like myself, traversed the desert of sand. It was destined to reach the ear of one its siblings, a migrant Iraqi child. And yet, what is more important than my position in this itinerary is the castle of 'Once Upon a Time' which, through its transcendence of time and place, has facilitated and hosted this meeting between two Iraqis, a child and song, in its bosom … and between its gazing bricks.

Turning left at the entrance, we are met with a meandering walkway and promenade that seems to stretch towards the very openness of outer space. This imaginative portrayal is facilitated by my own forgetfulness of the bricks which mold the body of the castle in this wing and the non-existent roof which constantly attracted the stygian magic of Jordanian nights into the ambiance of the castle. Like dark Arabian hair, these contenders of daytime dressed and veiled the castle's visitors and protected their privacy.

The march towards whatever end exists for this castle takes us towards boutiques that sell a myriad of things, from handmade natural soaps and rugs to freshly cooked glass and pottery. The close vicinity of each of these shops procured its own delicacy of breezes and ambiances. Between the natural smell of olives and blazing heat of the glass oven, I linger as the child who visited Kan Zaman countless times, never once taking care to commemorate a sojourn in writing for a séance like this … nor for the inevitable journey across time, space and pain towards the New World.

To be continued …